POSITIVE THINKING

FOR THE INTROVERT

Harness Optimism to Thrive
in an Extrovert World

CHLOE BRYANT

Unleash Your Introvert Power: Free Download!

Thank you for choosing *Positive Thinking for the Introvert: Harness Optimism to Thrive in an Extrovert World!* As a special gift, I'm offering you a downloadable list of "**Introvert Power: Positive Affirmations**" to help you cultivate self-compassion, embrace your strengths, and navigate social situations with confidence.

Here's what you'll get:

- A collection of powerful affirmations designed to boost your self-belief and empower you as an introvert.
- Daily reminders to challenge negative self-talk and cultivate a positive mindset.

How to Claim Your Free Gift:

Scan the QR code below or visit https://BookHip.com/WVJBAFT to download your "Introvert Power: Positive Affirmations" list.

Start affirming your inner strength today!

The best to you,

Chloe Bryant

CONTENTS

PREFACE

"In a gentle way, you can shake the world."

- Mahatma Gandhi

In this often loud and overwhelming world, the soft echoes of introversion are frequently drowned out. Yet it is these very whispers that carry the power to resonate deeply and effect meaningful change. Inspired by the insightful words of Mahatma Gandhi, this book embarks on a journey to shift the paradigms of thought, especially for the introverted soul navigating an extroverted society.

Crafted with care, the essence of this book unfolds across chapters that aim to empower the introverted individual. It draws from the well of positive psychology, offering a beacon of hope and a toolkit for thriving in a world that hasn't always understood the quiet strength of introversion. My purpose in writing this stems from a heartfelt desire to illuminate the path for my fellow introverts. I aim to embellish your world with optimism, helping you to harness your inherent strengths to live a life of fulfillment, confidence, and success.

Growing up as an introvert, I often found myself in the shadows, watching as the world seemed to cater to those more outspoken, those who shone brightly in the spotlight. It wasn't until I encountered individuals like you—talented, thoughtful, but struggling with self-doubt and societal pressures—that I recognized a universal plight and a spark within myself to contribute to a change. The stories of people who found it daunting to voice their ideas in a loud room or those who hesitated to step forward due to fear of rejection became the catalyst for this endeavor. It was in these shared experiences, these collective moments of hesitancy, that I found the impetus to write this book.

This journey has been paved with the insights of renowned psychologists, the wisdom of successful introverts who've made their mark, and the support of countless individuals who've shared their stories and struggles with me. It's their experiences, combined with my own, that have shaped the strategies and perspectives shared within these pages.

You, my reader, are at the heart of this journey. You've taken a brave step by picking up this book, choosing to invest your time and trust in my words. This gesture is not something I take lightly.

This book is for anyone who has ever felt like an observer in a world that doesn't stop talking. It's for the thoughtful, the reflective, and those who seek deep connections. There are no prerequisites for understanding the material—only a willingness to open your mind to the potential that lies within your quiet nature.

By the end of this book, you'll not only recognize introversion as the incredible strength it is but also possess the tools to foster a positive mindset and demolish the barriers of self-doubt and anxiety. You will be equipped to build genuine connections and seize opportunities with a newfound confidence.

Thank you for embarking on this journey with me. Together, we'll explore the realms of positive thinking, diving deep into how you, the introverted individual, can not only thrive but flourish in an extrovert world.

Continue reading, for at the end of this exploration lies the key to unlocking the boundless potential that quietly resides within you.

CHAPTER 1

THE SILENT
SUPERPOWER

In the still of the early morning, Eleanor sat by her bedroom window, the first soft light of dawn caressing her thoughtful face. She watched the dew-laden grass in her garden glisten, a silent observer to the awakening world. Today she had an interview, a chance to advance in a world where often the loud are heard and the quiet overlooked. Her heart in silent conference, she mulled over the quiet power that thrummed in her veins.

Eleanor was not one to command a room with volume, but with a presence born of listening, understanding, and deep introspection. She remembered moments when her silence had been mistaken for disinterest, her careful speech misconstrued for lack of confidence. But today, she resolved, would mark a different confluence.

The last conference had called for her expertise, and yet she had receded into the tapestried walls of the room, her voice lost in the chorus of more extroverted peers. They knew her work, the meticulous, saturated hours she poured into her projects, and yet her ideas remained like unsung melodies.

But Eleanor found solace in the knowledge that her introversion was not a flaw but a labyrinthine garden of thought where richer, deeper ideas bloomed. She recognized that her strength lay in the ability to work through problems with a focus that was undivided, her mind a well of carefully curated knowledge. Today she would be her own advocate, her quiet confidence a shield, her introspective wisdom a sword.

Disturbed by the chirp of a robin, Eleanor smiled. Nature did not hurry, and neither did she. At her very core, she knew her value, and she intended to project it not just in words, but in the poise and consideration of her arguments. The world thrived on balance, and she, like the robin's song that finds its way through the clutter of the morning rush, would make her presence felt amidst the din of extroverted norms.

As she gathered her thoughts and prepared to step into the day, Eleanor harbored no illusions about the challenge ahead. She pondered the endless possibilities that lay before her. Could the world truly embrace the quiet strength she carried, or would she once again need to prove that the deepest waters are often the most still?

UNLEASHING THE INTROVERT'S SUPERPOWER

In a world that can't stop talking, the whisper of the introvert rarely gets the amplification it deserves. Yet there's a dormant superpower within this whisper waiting to be harnessed. This might sound like a bold assertion, especially when society often equates success and leadership with extroversion. However, **keen observation skills, deep thinking, and focused work ethic** are just a few introverted qualities that hold immense potential for personal and professional success. The key lies in **shifting our perspective**—from viewing introversion as a limitation to celebrating it as a valuable trait.

11

Understanding the **Introverted Advantage** is the first step toward this shift. Introverts are not just good listeners; they are often excellent observers, capable of noticing subtleties that others might miss. This can be a game-changer in fields that require a keen eye for detail. Similarly, their tendency to think before they speak fosters **deep thinking**, enabling them to come up with well-considered solutions to complex problems. And when it comes to dedication, introverts often exhibit a **focused work ethic** that can lead to high-quality outcomes and innovation.

Society often paints introversion as a disadvantage, glorifying the charismatic and outgoing while overlooking the potential strengths that introverts bring to the table. However, it's time to challenge this narrative and recognize the superpowers that lie within every introvert:

1. Keen Observation Skills: Introverts possess an uncanny ability to notice the subtle nuances that others often miss. Their keen observation skills allow them to pick up on nonverbal cues, detect underlying patterns, and gain a deeper understanding of the world around them. In fields like research, journalism, and psychology, this skill is not just valuable—it's essential.

2. Deep Thinking: While extroverts may thrive on quick-fire brainstorming sessions, introverts excel in deep, introspective thinking. They have a natural inclination to delve into complex subjects, analyzing them from various angles and unearthing insights that others might overlook. This ability to think critically and creatively is a catalyst for innovation and problem-solving in any domain.

3. Focused Work Ethics: Introverts are at their best when they can work independently, immersing themselves fully in their tasks without the distractions of constant social stimulation. This ability to focus intensely for extended periods allows them to produce high-quality work and

develop a deep mastery of their chosen field. In a world where multitasking is often praised, the introvert's single-minded dedication is a rare and valuable asset.

By recognizing and harnessing these strengths, introverts can **reframe** their perceived weaknesses into powerful tools for success in both personal and professional settings.

As we navigate through these pages, keep in mind the overarching theme of **positive thinking**. It's a powerful tool that, when combined with the unique strengths of the introverted personality, can unlock doors to new possibilities. Whether in personal relationships, professional endeavors, or personal development, the potential for introverts to make a significant impact is immense. It's time to embrace this silent superpower and let it shine.

QUIET CONFIDENCE: THRIVING AS AN INTROVERT

Navigating an extrovert-centric world can be challenging for introverts, but with the right strategies and mindset, they can cultivate a quiet confidence that allows them to thrive.

Here are some strategies to help you develop on the path to self-assured success:

1. **Embrace your strengths**: The first step in building quiet confidence is to fully honor and celebrate your unique strengths as an introvert. Rather than trying to force yourself into an extroverted mold, focus on leveraging your natural abilities—your keen observation skills, deep thinking, and focused work ethic—to showcase your expertise and value.

2. **Build self-belief**: Developing self-belief is crucial for quiet confidence. Start by acknowledging your accomplishments and celebrating your successes, no matter how small they may seem. Remind yourself of the unique value you bring

to the table and the positive impact you have on those around you. Surround yourself with supportive people who believe in your abilities and can serve as a source of encouragement and inspiration.

3. **Challenge negative self-talk**: Introverts often fall into the trap of negative self-talk, constantly comparing themselves to their more outgoing counterparts. To break free from this cycle, make a conscious effort to replace self-limiting thoughts like "I'm too quiet" or "I'm not good enough" with empowering positive affirmations such as "My calm presence puts others at ease" or "My insights are valuable and worthy of being shared."

4. **Practice self-care**: Prioritizing self-care is essential for introverts to recharge and rejuvenate. Make time for activities and hobbies that bring you joy and help you unwind. Create boundaries and learn to say no when necessary to protect your energy. Taking care of yourself physically, emotionally, and mentally will strengthen your confidence and resilience.

5. **Practice assertive communication**: While introverts may prefer listening to speaking, developing assertive communication skills is crucial for expressing ideas and needs with clarity and confidence. Start by practicing active listening, focusing on understanding others before formulating your response. When it's your turn to speak, take a moment to gather your thoughts and then express yourself calmly and directly, maintaining eye contact and open body language.

6. **Seek opportunities for growth**: Quiet confidence is not built in a vacuum; it's forged through experiences that push us beyond our comfort zones. Cultivate opportunities for growth by taking on new projects at work, joining professional organizations, or attending networking events. While these situations may feel daunting initially,

each successful encounter will boost your self-assurance and expand your skillset in meaningful ways.

7. **Celebrate your introverted nature**: Instead of viewing introversion as a limitation, acknowledge it as a valuable trait that contributes to your success. Recognize the unique insights and perspectives you bring to the table, and don't shy away from sharing your thoughts and ideas. Celebrate the moments of solitude and reflection that allow you to recharge and come up with innovative solutions. By honoring and celebrating your introverted nature, you can cultivate a sense of quiet confidence that shines from within.

Remember, quiet confidence is not about trying to be someone you're not or becoming more extroverted. It is about nurturing your authentic self, recognizing your strengths, and navigating the world with authenticity and assertiveness. By developing quiet confidence, introverts can thrive and find success and fulfillment in any sphere of life.

REAL-WORLD SUCCESS: INTROVERTS MAKING A DIFFERENCE

Throughout history, introverts have made groundbreaking contributions across various fields, proving that quiet strength can yield remarkable results. Consider these inspiring examples:

- Rosa Parks, the iconic civil rights activist, demonstrated the power of quiet resilience when she refused to give up her bus seat, sparking a movement that would change the course of American history. Her calm determination in the face of adversity exemplifies the introvert's ability to effect change through principled action.
- Bill Gates, the co-founder of Microsoft, leveraged his deep thinking and laser-focused work ethic to revolutionize the tech industry. His ability to immerse himself in complex

problems and develop innovative solutions transformed personal computing and set the stage for the digital age.

- J.K. Rowling, the acclaimed author of the Harry Potter series, harnessed her rich inner world and vivid imagination to create a literary phenomenon that captivated readers around the globe. Her success is a testament to the introvert's capacity for profound creativity and storytelling.

THE QUIET REVOLUTION: CHANGING THE NARRATIVE

As more introverts begin to recognize and harness their unique strengths, a quiet revolution is unfolding—one that challenges the long-held belief that extroversion is the key to success. By reframing introversion as a valuable asset, we can create a more inclusive and diverse world that celebrates the contributions of all personality types.

This shift in perspective is not just beneficial for introverts; it's essential for society as a whole. In a rapidly changing world filled with complex challenges, we need the deep thinkers, the keen observers, and the focused problem-solvers that introverts embody. By fostering a positive culture that values and nurtures these qualities, we can unlock untold potential and drive innovation in every field.

Now that you've examined the realm of introversion and uncovered its hidden potential, it's time to step into your own light and *embrace* your introverted superpower. Remember, your unique strengths are not limitations but powerful tools that can propel you to success and fulfillment. Let's recap the key insights we've uncovered in this chapter:

1. **The Introverted Advantage**: Your unique strengths as an introvert, such as keen observation skills, deep thinking abilities, and a focused work ethic, set you apart in a world that often favors extroversion.

2. **Reframing Introversion**: By recognizing and valuing introverted traits in both personal and professional settings, you can leverage your natural inclinations to thrive and excel.

3. **Quiet Confidence**: The strategies we've explored will help you harness your introverted qualities for success, build self-belief, and challenge negative stereotypes about introversion.

LOOK FORWARD TO WHAT LIES AHEAD

As you embark on the journey through the pages of this book to harness your introverted power, optimism and positivity, know that you are not alone. Countless successful introverts have walked this path before you, leaving a trail of inspiration and proof that quiet strength can move mountains. So welcome your authentic self, let your inner light shine, and watch as you make your mark on the world in your own beautifully understated way.

NEXT UP

Now that you've championed your introverted superpower, you might be surprised by a persistent voice whispering negativity. This inner critic can hold you back from fully unleashing your potential. In the next chapter, we'll dig into strategies for silencing this self-doubt and harnessing the full power of your introverted strengths.

CHAPTER 2

REWIRING
YOUR INNER CRITIC

Thomas walked through the chilled autumn air, a misting rain clinging to the shoulders of his jacket like a persistent memory. The gray overcast sky droned on dull and uninspiring as he made his way along the river walk, his mind tussling with unwelcome thoughts that seemed to burrow deeper like uninvited guests.

He was haunted by a relentless inner critic, a voice spawning from the depths of his insecurity which murmured falsehoods, berating him for his perceived inadequacies. Today, the specter of a past failure at work inflamed his self-critique, hashing and rehashing a presentation gone awry. With each echo of negative self-talk, his shoulders hunched as if bracing against a physical blow.

In the midst of his contemplation, a child's laughter sliced through the oppressive mood, challenging his gloomy thoughts. Nearby, a boy skipped stones across the river, reveling in his successes and unaffected by those that merely plunked and sank. Perhaps there was a lesson to be learned by that unbridled optimism.

Thomas turned away from the river and meandered into a pocket park, where yellowed leaves danced at his feet, each step crunching a verse of upheaval. He recalled an article he had read on challenging cognitive distortions, resolving to apply its techniques. "Identify the distortion," he recited inwardly. "Look for evidence. Is it true? What are the odds?" His stride grew firmer with this newfound resolve.

Crossing the park, he found a secluded bench and sat, a tableau of people bustling around him, each wrapped in their own narratives. He drew a deep breath of the air laced with the musty scent of damp earth. Words he had once heard, words of affirmation, seemed to rise within him like a spring whispered by the earth. "I am capable," he told himself. "I learn and grow from my challenges."

Committing to this practice, he decided to infuse his daily life with these mantras. The mere act of speaking positivity rippled within him, a pebble of hope in a lake of doubts.

Nearby, squirrels performed acrobatics among the branches, their playful abandon a testament to the resilience woven into the fabric of nature. Watching them, Thomas pondered his own capacity to cultivate such resilience. What exercises could he weave into the fabric of his daily life to reinforce this new vision of himself?

A sense of determination seeped into his veins, warming him against the autumn chill. He would no longer be a passive listener to his internal narrative. He would script affirmations of his worth, etch them into his daily consciousness, decluttering his thoughts as one by one, the leaves around him dropped from their branches in a cycle of renewal.

As he observed the world moving through its paces—the symphony of life in its ruckus and revelation—he wondered: Could these small, positive refrains be the key to turn the lock on a door that led to a more optimistic and resilient life?

TAMING YOUR INNER CRITIC: TRANSFORMING THE VOICE IN YOUR HEAD

You know that voice in your head that just won't quit? The one that's always pointing out your flaws and making you second-guess yourself? Yeah, that's your inner critic. We've all got one, and let me tell you, it can be a real buzz kill. It's a familiar, and often unwelcome, guest in the chambers of our minds. But the good news is we don't have to let it control the conversation.

This chapter will equip you with the tools to rewire your inner critic and transform it into your biggest cheerleader. Here, we'll embark on a journey to silence the negativity and cultivate a more positive inner dialogue.

UNVEILING THE ANTAGONIST: RECOGNIZING NEGATIVE SELF-TALK

The first step to silencing our inner critic is recognizing its tactics. Think of it like identifying a manipulative acquaintance. Once you understand its tricks, you can start to counter them. Here are some common ways our inner critic likes to sabotage us:

- **All-or-Nothing Thinking:** This distorts our perspective, forcing us to view situations in extremes. It's either a perfect success or a complete failure. This leaves no room for nuance or the possibility of learning from mistakes.
- **Overgeneralization:** We take one negative event and blow it out of proportion, making it a reflection of our entire worth. A bad presentation doesn't mean you're a terrible speaker; it just means you might need to practice more.
- **Mental Filtering:** Our inner critic is a master at selective attention. It focuses solely on the negative aspects of a situation, conveniently filtering out any positive elements.

Did you receive ten positive comments on your work and one negative one? The critic will relentlessly highlight the negative one.

- **Mind-Reading:** We fall prey to the illusion of knowing exactly what others are thinking, and it's never good news. Our inner critic convinces us everyone is judging us harshly, even when there's no evidence to support it.
- **Emotional Reasoning:** We confuse our emotions with facts. Feeling anxious about a presentation doesn't necessarily mean you're going to fail. It just means you care about doing well.

By recognizing these patterns, we begin to see the inner critic for what it is: a voice fueled by negativity and distortion.

TAKING BACK CONTROL: CHALLENGING NEGATIVE THOUGHTS

Now that we've identified the inner critic's tactics, it's time to fight back! Here are some effective strategies to challenge those negative thoughts and reclaim control of your inner dialogue:

- **Question the Evidence:** Don't blindly accept your negative thoughts as truth. Ask yourself, "Is there any real evidence to support this?" Often, the critic relies on assumptions and worst-case scenarios rather than facts.
- **Challenge the Distortion:** Identify the cognitive distortion behind the negative thought. Are you engaging in all-or-nothing thinking, over-generalizing, or mind reading? Once you recognize the distortion, you can begin to reframe the thought in a more balanced and realistic way.
- **Offer a More Balanced Perspective:** Look at the situation objectively. What are the actual facts? What are you overlooking because of your heightened negativity?

BUILDING YOUR CONFIDENCE: THE POWER OF POSITIVE AFFIRMATIONS

Positive affirmations are like daily vitamins for your self-esteem. They're short, positive statements that can help counteract negative self-talk and reinforce your strengths. Here's how to make affirmations work for you:

- **Personalize Your Power Statements:** Craft affirmations that resonate with your specific goals and values. Instead of a generic "I am good enough," try something like "I am a capable and worthy writer," or "I am a strong and resilient learner."

- **Present Tense is Your Friend:** Frame your affirmations in the present tense as if the positive quality you're affirming is already true. "I am confident" has a stronger impact than "I will be confident someday."

- **Repetition is Key:** Affirmations work best when they become a regular habit. Repeat them daily, whether it's out loud in the morning, silently throughout the day, or written down in a journal.

- **Combine with Visualization:** To enhance the effectiveness of your affirmations, combine them with visualization and action. Visualize yourself embodying the qualities and abilities you are affirming and take action toward your goals. By combining these practices, you are reinforcing your affirmations with powerful mental imagery and physical steps toward your desired outcomes.

- **Get Creative:** Make affirmations enjoyable! Write them on colorful sticky notes and place them where you'll see them often—your bathroom mirror, fridge, or even your phone case. The more you see them, the more they'll start to sink in.

CULTIVATING OPTIMISM AND RESILIENCE: EMBRACING CHALLENGES

Life throws curveballs—that's a given. But with a positive mindset, you're better equipped to handle them and bounce back stronger. Here are some tips to cultivate optimism and resilience:

- **Reframe Challenges as Opportunities:** View setbacks as stepping stones on your path to growth. Did you bomb a job interview? Consider it a learning experience—an opportunity to refine your interview skills for the next one.
- **Focus on Your Strengths:** When faced with a challenge, take stock of your abilities and talents. What are you good at? Identifying your strengths can boost your confidence and help you approach the challenge with a sense of empowerment.
- **Practice Self-Compassion:** Be kind to yourself. Everyone makes mistakes and experiences setbacks. Don't let your inner critic use a challenge as an excuse for harsh self-criticism. Offer yourself understanding and encouragement just as you would to a friend.
- **Visualize Success:** Take a moment to imagine yourself achieving your goal or overcoming the challenge. What does it look and feel like? Engaging in positive visualization can boost your motivation and focus.

By consistently challenging your inner critic, using positive affirmations, and adopting a growth mindset, you'll cultivate a more optimistic and resilient outlook. Remember, this is a journey, not a destination. There will be days when the inner critic is louder than usual. Don't be discouraged by setbacks. Celebrate your progress, no matter how small, and keep moving forward.

TAKING ACTION: PUTTING IT ALL TOGETHER

The strategies we've discussed are powerful tools, but lasting change requires consistent effort. Here are some tips for integrating these practices into your daily routine:

- **Schedule Time for Reflection:** Set aside 10-15 minutes each day to reflect on your thoughts and feelings. Notice any patterns of negative self-talk and challenge them using the techniques we've discussed.
- **Start Your Day with Affirmations:** Begin your day by repeating your affirmations out loud or writing them down in a journal. This sets a positive tone for the day and reminds you of your strengths and goals.
- **Practice Gratitude:** Take time each day to appreciate the good things in your life, big or small. Gratitude journaling is a powerful way to cultivate a more positive outlook.
- **Surround Yourself with Positivity:** Seek out supportive friends and mentors who believe in you and encourage you. Minimize your exposure to negativity and people who drain your energy.
- **Track Your Progress**: Keep a journal to record your thoughts, challenges and victories as you work toward rewiring your inner critic.

By making these practices a regular part of your life, you'll gradually rewire your inner critic and transform it into a source of encouragement and support. Remember, the voice in your head has immense power. Don't let it be a constant source of negativity. Take control, silence the critic, and cultivate a positive inner dialogue that empowers you to thrive.

REMEMBER, EVERY STEP COUNTS!

As you continue on your path of self-discovery and growth, know that every small effort you make toward challenging negative self-talk and embracing positive affirmations is a step in the right direction.

Believe in your ability to transform your mindset and navigate life's challenges with resilience and optimism. You have the power to shape your inner narrative and create a more empowering reality.

YOUR OPTIMISTIC FUTURE AWAITS!

With each positive affirmation, you are laying the foundation for a brighter, more confident self. Embrace this journey of self-transformation with openness and determination.

Trust in the process, stay committed to your growth, and celebrate every triumph along the way. Your optimistic future is within reach, waiting for you to claim it!

NEXT UP

Feeling overwhelmed and stuck in a cycle of procrastination? Chapter 3 dives into the psychology of procrastination and explores practical strategies to get things done and stop feeling bogged down by tasks. We'll equip you with the tools to overcome procrastination and achieve your goals with greater efficiency and focus. So turn the page and let's tackle this challenge together!

CHAPTER 3

BREAKING THE PROCRASTINATION SPELL

O n a mellow Thursday afternoon, the sun hung low in the sky above a quaint garden terrace where Michael found himself seated, a notepad resting on the wooden table before him. Tiny birds flitted between the hedges, their songs punctuating the subtle rustle of leaves.

He squinted at the list of tasks scrawled upon the page, the sheer volume overwhelming. A long sigh escaped him, one drawn from the well of countless sighs before. His mind flirted with the seductive urge to delay, to defer until tomorrow what the sun today still had the time to witness. Michael questioned if he were simply lazy, but a sharper voice chided him from within. It wasn't laziness; it was fear, dressed in the garb of an aim for perfection— this relentless captor that had named itself Procrastination.

The memory of his mentor's advice echoed as he considered the first task. "Break it down, Michael, as one would dismantle a monolith, piece by piece." He drew little circles next to each step, dividing the monster before him into smaller, less daunting creatures. The terracotta pot beside him, with its singular daisy reaching for the sky, seemed to smile in approval.

With furrowed brow, he envisioned the project's completion. There was sweetness to the thought, an uplift in the chest at the imagined pride of a task well done. Could he harness this joy, this fleeting glimpse of satisfaction? The chirping of a robin provided a rhythmic backdrop as his pen started scratching against the paper, each mark a tiny victory sown.

Each circle filled brought him closer to that exuberant lightness he knew awaited him at the journey's end. There was strength in his quiet resolve, an introverted fortitude that carried him through the labyrinth of his doubts. He breathed in the fragrance of blooming lavender, letting the sensory peace bolster his spirit.

Was his meticulous mind, so prone to the pitfalls of over-thought, capable of embracing this new perspective? Could it lead to a renewed sense of self, one that celebrated incremental triumphs and appreciated the steady pace of progress over the headlong rush to completion? Could the world around him, with its expectations and feverish pace, understand the deep triumph in his silent battles?

UNDERSTANDING THE PROCRASTINATION PUZZLE:

The sinking feeling of an approaching deadline, the ever-growing to-do list, the paralyzing fear of failure—procrastination is a familiar foe for many. Often misinterpreted as laziness, it's a complex phenomenon rooted in our internal narratives and emotions. It's a universal challenge, especially in today's world that prioritizes constant productivity. However, for introverts, the pressure to constantly "be on" can exacerbate procrastination tendencies.

The key lies in **reframing procrastination**, not as a character flaw, but as a symptom of deeper issues. It could be fear of failure, perfectionism, or negative self-talk holding you back. Let's meet Sarah, an introverted writer who constantly procrastinates on finishing her novel. The looming deadline and fear of judgment trigger perfectionist tendencies, making her rewrite scenes endlessly. Recognizing this pattern as fear, not laziness, allows Sarah to address the root cause.

Identifying the root causes of procrastination requires introspection. Through exercises like **journaling** or **creating a mind map**, individuals can uncover the underlying fears or beliefs fueling their procrastination. This revelation is empowering, enabling a targeted approach to overcoming procrastination.

WHY PROCRASTINATION THRIVES IN INTROVERTED MINDS

Introverts gain energy from solitude and focused work. External stimulation, like constant social interaction or overwhelming deadlines, can be draining. This can create a vicious cycle with procrastination. Feeling overwhelmed by a task, an introvert might withdraw, which then fuels procrastination, leading to even greater overwhelm and a sense of failure. While it's a universal struggle, introverts often find themselves facing a double whammy. Their natural tendencies can create a breeding ground for procrastination. Here's a deeper look:

1. Stimulation Overload:

- **Introverts gain energy from solitude and focused work.** Loud environments, constant meetings, or open-plan offices can be draining. This can lead to feeling overwhelmed by tasks, making them even less appealing to tackle.
- **Imagine David, an introverted graphic designer.** Deadlines approach, but brainstorming sessions with his extroverted colleagues leave him feeling drained and needing quiet time to recharge. This can make starting the actual design work feel daunting.

2. The Perfectionism Trap:

- **Introverts often have a strong internal compass and a desire to do things well.** This can morph into perfectionism, where the fear of not doing something perfectly leads to complete avoidance.
- **Think about Sarah, an introverted writer.** She has a brilliant novel brewing in her head, but the fear of not crafting the perfect opening sentence keeps her from putting pen to paper (or fingers to keyboard).

3. The Decision Fatigue Drain:

- **Introverts tend to be more analytical and deliberate in their decision-making.** Constant choices, even small ones, can deplete their mental energy. This can make starting a complex task, which often involves multiple decisions, feel overwhelming.
- **Take Michael, an introverted software developer.** He needs to tackle a major coding project, but just deciding which programming language to use and setting up his development environment feels like a hurdle, leading him to browse social media instead.

4. The Introverted Recharge Myth:

- **There's a misconception that introverts are simply shy or antisocial.** While they may need to recharge after social interaction, introverts also crave connection and enjoy socializing—just in smaller doses and with close friends or family.
- **Consider Emily, an introverted accountant.** She loves spending time with her book club friends, but large social gatherings leave her feeling depleted. The pressure to socialize after a long workweek can make her procrastinate on her errands and chores, leading to a last-minute scramble.

Understanding these reasons is the first step to overcoming procrastination as an introvert. The good news is, your introverted strengths can also be powerful tools for conquering this challenge.

EVICTING PROCRASTINATION: STRATEGIES FOR INTROVERTED MINDS

Understanding why procrastination thrives in introverted minds is crucial, but the real power lies in actionable strategies. Here's how you, as an introvert, can combat procrastination and reclaim your productivity:

1. Tame the Stimulation Beast:

- **Create a dedicated workspace:** Find a quiet corner at home, utilize the local library, or invest in co-working space with designated quiet zones. Minimize distractions with noise-canceling headphones or white noise machines.
- **Communicate boundaries:** Let colleagues or housemates know when you need uninterrupted work time. Schedule focused work sessions in your calendar and treat them like important appointments.
- **Batch similar tasks:** Group tasks that require similar levels of focus together. This minimizes the decision fatigue associated with switching between tasks with different requirements.

Example: David, the graphic designer, can schedule focused design sessions in a quiet co-working space, letting his colleagues know he needs uninterrupted time. Batching brainstorming sessions with solo design work can also help him manage stimulation overload.

2. Perfectionism? More Like Progress-ion!

- **Embrace imperfection:** First drafts don't have to be perfect, presentations don't have to be flawless. Focus on progress, not perfection.
- **Set realistic goals:** Break down large, daunting tasks into smaller, achievable chunks. Celebrate completing each step as a mini-victory.
- **Challenge your inner critic:** When negative self-talk creeps in, reframe it. Instead of "This is never going to be good enough," say "I'm learning and growing with each step."

Example: Sarah, the writer, can set a daily writing goal of 500 words instead of trying to write the perfect opening chapter. Finishing each day with 500 words under her belt creates a sense of accomplishment and keeps her moving forward.

3. Decision Fatigue? Make Choices Your Ally:

- **Plan your day the night before:** Knowing what tasks need to be tackled minimizes the decision fatigue of "what to do next" in the morning.
- **Create templates and routines:** Develop templates for frequently used documents or emails to avoid wasting time reinventing the wheel each time.
- **Utilize decision-making tools:** Use a daily planner or project management app to organize tasks and prioritize your workload.

Example: Michael, the software developer, can plan his coding project the night before, outlining the specific tasks he wants to accomplish. Using a project management app can help him visualize the steps involved and avoid feeling overwhelmed.

4. Recharge, Reconnect, Repeat:

- **Schedule social time strategically:** Plan social outings for times when you feel most energized, leaving ample quiet recharge time before and after.
- **Communicate your needs:** Suggest activities that allow for deeper conversations rather than large, loud gatherings.
- **Embrace "alone time" activities:** Schedule time for hobbies and activities you find energizing, whether it's reading in a quiet corner, spending time in nature, or indulging in a relaxing bath.

Example: Emily, the accountant, can schedule her book club meetings for weekend afternoons when she feels most social. Letting her friends know she needs some quiet time after work allows her to recharge before the next social interaction.

Remember, these are just a few strategies. Experiment and find what works best for you. By understanding your introverted strengths and implementing these tips, you can overcome procrastination and build a fulfilling life that respects your need for focused work and quiet recharge.

The next section will introduce the Introverted Action-Oriented Procrastination Model (IAPM)—a framework designed to help you leverage your unique strengths and create a system for productivity and fulfillment.

THE IAPM: YOUR PERSONALIZED ANTI-PROCRASTINATION TOOLKIT

The **Introverted Action-Oriented Procrastination Model (IAPM)** offers a framework to harness your introverted strengths and create a productive workflow that respects your need for focused work and quiet recharge. Here's how the IAPM can help you:

1. Motivation Through Reflection: Aligning Tasks with Values

Introverts often find intrinsic motivation more compelling than external pressures. Take Emily, an introverted accountant. Tax season is a period of intense work, but Emily finds it easier to power through when she reflects on how her work helps families plan for their future. This sense of purpose fuels her motivation.

To utilize this strength, take time to journal about the task at hand. Ask yourself: "How does completing this task align with my values and long-term goals?" Is it a stepping stone toward your dream job? Does it contribute to your financial security? Connecting tasks to your core values injects them with meaning and makes them feel less like burdens.

Putting It into Practice:

Let's revisit Michael, the software developer. He struggles with procrastination on a crucial project presentation. By using the IAPM's reflection prompt, he realizes that delivering a successful presentation will not only impress his colleagues but also contribute to the overall success of the project, something he deeply cares about. This newfound sense of purpose motivates him to start tackling the presentation in manageable steps.

2. Task Breakdown and Engagement: Taming the To-Do List Monster

Introverts excel at meticulous planning and focused attention. Use this strength by creating a detailed action plan. Break down overwhelming tasks into smaller, achievable chunks. For example, instead of facing the daunting task of "write a book proposal," break it down into smaller steps like "research target publishers," "develop a compelling synopsis," and so on. Seeing the progress on smaller tasks builds momentum and reduces overwhelm.

Another effective strategy in breaking down tasks is creating a to-do list. Writing down the individual steps needed to complete a task helps bring clarity and structure to the process. It allows you to prioritize your tasks and focus on the most important ones. Plus, there's the added satisfaction of crossing items off your list as they are completed. Breaking down tasks in this way helps prevent feelings of overwhelm and provides a clear path forward.

Visualization can also be a powerful tool in breaking down tasks. Close your eyes and imagine yourself completing each step of the task, visualizing yourself navigating through each stage with ease and confidence. By mentally rehearsing the process, you familiarize yourself with the task and reduce anxiety. This technique can be especially helpful for introverts who may prefer internal visualization over external action.

Leveraging Your Strengths:

Remember Sarah, the writer? After acknowledging her fear of judgment, she starts tackling smaller writing goals. She creates a daily schedule that allocates specific time slots for focused writing sessions. Knowing she only needs to focus for a set amount of time helps her overcome the initial inertia. She also breaks down the novel writing process into smaller tasks like character development, scene outlining, and dialogue writing. Completing these smaller tasks provides a sense of accomplishment and keeps her motivated.

3. Reward and Reflection: Celebrating Small Wins

Celebrating milestones, no matter how small, is crucial. Introverts often find quiet forms of self-reward most satisfying. After completing a task segment, take a moment to reflect on your accomplishment. Did you learn something new? Did you overcome a challenge? Maybe reward yourself with a cup of tea and some quiet reading time in your favorite corner.

The Power of Positive Reinforcement:

Research shows that positive reinforcement is a powerful tool for building habits and overcoming procrastination. By rewarding yourself for completing tasks, you create a positive association with work, making it more likely you'll tackle similar tasks in the future.

4. Building Momentum with the Introverted Advantage:

Introverts have a natural tendency for deep focus and sustained concentration. Leverage this strength by creating a dedicated workspace that minimizes distractions. This could be a quiet corner in your home, a local library, or even a rented co-working space with designated quiet zones.

Creating Your Sanctuary:

Equip your workspace with tools that enhance focus, such as noise-canceling headphones or white noise machines. Let colleagues or housemates know when you need uninterrupted work time. Utilize time management techniques like the Pomodoro Technique, which involves working in focused 25-minute intervals with short breaks in between.

The Power of Planning and Scheduling:

Introverts often thrive on routine and predictability. Schedule specific times for focused work in your calendar and treat these appointments with the same respect you would a client meeting. This helps you mentally prepare for deep work sessions and minimizes the decision fatigue that can lead to procrastination.

5. Embracing Imperfection and Self-Compassion:

Perfectionism is a common culprit behind procrastination for introverts. The fear of not doing something perfectly can lead to complete avoidance. The key is to accept imperfection and practice self-compassion. Remember, the first draft doesn't have to be perfect, the presentation doesn't have to be flawless—progress, not perfection, is the goal.

Challenge Your Inner Critic:

When negative self-talk creeps in, challenge those thoughts. Instead of saying, "This is never going to be good enough," reframe it as "I'm learning and growing with each step." Forgive yourself for setbacks and view them as opportunities for improvement.

Building Self-Confidence:

Self-compassion and celebrating small wins build self-confidence. As you start completing tasks and overcoming challenges, you'll develop a belief in your abilities. This newfound confidence further fuels your motivation and reduces the fear of failure that can trigger procrastination.

The Cycle of Introverted Productivity:

The IAPM emphasizes a cyclical nature of motivation and engagement. There will be ups and downs. When motivation dips, revisit your reflection on the task's value (Step 1) or break down a larger task into even smaller steps (Step 2). Remember, every completed step is a success. Take Sarah, the writer, again. After acknowledging her fear of judgment, she starts tackling smaller writing goals, celebrating each completed chapter with a relaxing bath—a reward that fuels her motivation to keep going.

BEYOND PROCRASTINATION: BUILDING A FULFILLING LIFE AS AN INTROVERT

Conquering procrastination is just one step toward a fulfilling life as an introvert. Understanding and embracing your introverted nature is key. Introverts need time for solitude and quiet reflection to recharge their energy. Don't feel pressured to constantly socialize or attend draining events. Prioritize activities that energize you, like spending time in nature, pursuing hobbies, or engaging in meaningful conversations with close friends.

BUILDING A SUPPORTIVE NETWORK:

Surround yourself with supportive people who understand and respect your introverted needs. Communicate your boundaries and recharge needs openly and honestly. Building a strong support system can help you navigate social situations without feeling drained.

THE JOY OF COMPLETION

Procrastination is not a reflection of your worth as an introvert. By understanding the root causes, leveraging your strengths with the IAPM framework, and practicing self-compassion, you can overcome procrastination and build a productive and fulfilling life that respects your unique needs. *The joy of completion doesn't have to wait until the end; it can be found in every step you take toward your goals.* **Acknowledge your progress, pat yourself on the back, and enjoy the journey of growth and achievement.** Remember, the journey is about progress, not perfection. Celebrate your small wins, receive your introverted nature, and thrive on your own terms.

NEXT UP

You've conquered a significant hurdle by overcoming procrastination and building a system that works for your introverted strengths. But for many introverts, navigating a world that often prioritizes constant social interaction can be another energy-depleting challenge.

In the next chapter, we'll shift gears to explore the art of managing your social energy and look at strategies for creating a comfortable social environment, understanding your introvert's recharge needs, and thriving in a world that favors extroversion without compromising your authenticity. Learn how to gracefully excuse yourself from draining situations, set healthy boundaries with friends and family, and find social interactions that energize you, not deplete you. With the tools from this chapter, you can build a fulfilling social life that respects your introverted nature and allows you to shine on your own terms.

Take a deep breath, introvert warrior! You've got this. With the strategies outlined in this chapter and the upcoming exploration of social serenity in Chapter 4, you're well on your way to building a life that allows you to thrive as the introverted powerhouse you are.

CHAPTER 4

CRAFTING
SOCIAL SERENITY

Luke sat solitary at the cliff edge, the sky a deepening shade of twilight blue, the horizon kissed by a slipping sun. He felt the coastal wind brush his face, the tang of salt on his lips. He pondered the art of conversation. His mind was a turbulent sea of thoughts, each wave crashing against the next—active listening, empathy, insightful questioning—a mantra for connection he struggled to embody. Alone amidst the symphony of whispering grass and the distant cries of seagulls, he sensed his barriers like the cliffs behind him: monumental and steep.

This evening was not unlike many others, except for the fold of paper from his pocket, creased with resolve. An invitation: a gathering, friends, laughter, shared stories. He recalled past attempts, the muffled words, the strained smiles, and how he'd retreated into shadowy corners, his presence shrinking until he became part of the furniture, unnoticed, silent. Would tonight be any different? Could he navigate the turbulent social waters that left him with a silent tongue?

Luke closed his eyes; he searched his heart for the bonds he yearned to strengthen. And as the ebb and flow of fear and longing battled within, he took solace in the knowledge that he needn't fill the air with empty chatter. *Quality over quantity*, his inner voice comforted. Fewer words, but each heavy with meaning, like stones skipped across the surface, causing ripples—his introverted tendencies were not a shackle but a key.

There was strength in genuine communication. He desired conversations that dived deep, that explored the ocean beds of shared human experience. Strong bonds were his lifeline, the ropes that would tether him to others amidst life's storms. Setting personal boundaries and practicing active listening, he reminded himself, would let those bonds form without fear of losing himself to the tempest.

As the sun dipped beneath its blanket of water, the stars began their silent vigil. Luke rose, the invitation now warm in his palm. His heart raced like a gull in flight, seeking its kin. He faced the cool night air—the taste of salt now a promise of a life filled with authentic engagements, real and imagined.

He stepped from the cliff's edge, his journey back to the warmth of hearth and shared humanity beginning with the crunch of gravel beneath his feet. The night wrapped him in its embrace, comforting in its vastness, a canvas for the possibilities that would unfold.

Would he find his voice, his tribe, among the laughter and warmth of a gathering that awaited him?

UNLOCKING THE SECRETS TO SOCIAL FULFILLMENT

In a world where everyone's glued to their phones and social media reigns supreme, having a real, heart-to-heart conversation can feel like a lost art. But here's the thing: deep down, we all still crave those meaningful connections. It's what makes us human, you know? This insight lays the groundwork for transforming how we approach our social interactions, especially for those of us who consider ourselves introverts in an environment that prizes socializing. The truth is, deep, meaningful conversations are akin to hidden treasures in the realm of social connections, significantly more valuable than a plethora of shallow exchanges. By focusing on quality over quantity, we open the door to forming stronger, more resilient bonds that are built on a foundation of genuine understanding and empathy.

Among the first steps to mastering this approach is honing the **Art of Conversation**. This involves improving our communication skills by emphasizing active listening, showing empathy, and asking insightful questions. For many of us, the idea of diving into deep conversations, particularly if we lean toward introversion, can seem daunting. However, by navigating social interactions with a toolkit designed to reduce anxiety and foster genuine exchanges, the process becomes not only manageable but enjoyable. Active listening, for instance, is not just about hearing words but about truly understanding the speaker's intentions, feelings, and messages. It's about showing genuine interest, which in return encourages openness and shared vulnerability.

Quality over Quantity in our social interactions allows us to leverage our introverted tendencies for greater depth in conversations. Introverts often possess a natural inclination toward thoughtful interaction, making them uniquely equipped to engage in meaningful dialogue. By focusing on fewer but richer conversations, we can create a space where authentic intimacy thrives. It's about embracing our natural predispositions and turning what might feel like a social drawback into our most potent tool for connecting with others on a profound level.

Imagine attending a friend's birthday party where you only know a handful of people. Instead of feeling overwhelmed by the crowd, you spot someone sitting alone and strike up a conversation. By asking thoughtful questions and showing genuine interest in their responses, you discover a shared passion for a particular hobby.

This quality interaction leads to a newfound friendship and a sense of belonging at the event.

Central to building and maintaining these impactful relationships is developing the skill to **Build Strong Bonds**. This means not only initiating genuine conversations but also setting personal boundaries, practicing empathy, and maintaining an ongoing commitment to active listening. These elements serve as the pillars for establishing authentic engagements that endure. Setting boundaries allows us to engage in interactions that feel safe and respectful, while empathy enables us to connect with others on an emotional level, fostering a sense of mutual understanding and support.

Throughout this journey, it's equally important to remember that moments of awkwardness or misunderstanding are part of the process of building deeper connections. It's in these moments that our willingness to be vulnerable, to share our own stories and listen to those of others truly shines. And it's here, in the sharing of our imperfections and the unguarded exploration of the lives of others, that we find the most potent connections.

Moreover, in this chapter, we'll explore practical strategies that address common challenges in social interactions. From dealing with social exhaustion to overcoming the fear of opening up, these strategies are designed to empower you to navigate your social world with greater ease and confidence. By implementing these actionable tips, you'll find yourself not only engaging in more meaningful conversations but also enjoying the process of getting there.

Ultimately, the pursuit of social serenity is about more than just avoiding shallow chatter. It's about cultivating a garden of relationships where authenticity, understanding, and empathy bloom. By prioritizing the quality of our interactions over their quantity, we unlock the door to a more fulfilling social life, one deep conversation at a time. And remember, in this journey of crafting social serenity, it's the small, consistent steps that lead to the most significant changes. By applying these principles in our daily lives, we not only enhance our own well-being but also contribute to a kinder, more connected world.

In a world dominated by constant digital chatter and superficial interactions, the art of conversation has lost some of its luster. Many of us find ourselves engaging in countless shallow exchanges, leaving us feeling unsatisfied, disconnected, and longing for deeper connections. So how can we reclaim the power of conversation and cultivate meaningful interactions in our lives?

It begins with active listening. When we truly listen to someone, we show them that we value their thoughts and opinions. We give them a safe space to express themselves fully, which in turn fosters trust and understanding. Instead of merely waiting for our turn to speak, we can practice active listening by fully focusing on the speaker, maintaining eye contact, and responding thoughtfully.

Empathy is also key to enhancing communication skills. By putting ourselves in someone else's shoes, we can better understand their perspective and respond in a way that validates their feelings and experiences. Empathy allows us to connect on a deeper level, creating an environment of compassion and mutual respect.

Asking insightful questions is another powerful tool in our conversational arsenal. Instead of settling for surface-level discussions, we can dive deeper by asking open-ended questions that encourage reflection and introspection. By showing a genuine interest in others and asking meaningful questions, we invite honest and authentic conversations that have the potential to transform our relationships.

Navigating social interactions can be anxiety-inducing for many introverts. The pressure to make small talk and constantly engage can leave us feeling exhausted and overwhelmed. However, by prioritizing quality over quantity in our conversations, we can alleviate some of this anxiety. Instead of trying to have a hundred interactions in a day, we can focus on having a few meaningful conversations that leave us feeling energized and fulfilled.

Key Points:

1. Active listening is a powerful tool in enhancing communication skills and building deeper connections.
2. Empathy allows us to understand and support others, fostering trust and mutual respect.
3. Asking insightful questions encourages meaningful conversations and invites reflection.
4. Prioritizing quality over quantity in our conversations can reduce anxiety and make interactions more meaningful.

So how can we put these strategies into action? How can we navigate social interactions with less anxiety and create space for deeper, more fulfilling conversations?

One practical tip is to set an intention before entering a social situation. By reminding ourselves to focus on actively listening, being empathetic, and asking insightful questions, we can approach conversations with purpose and direction.

Another strategy is to find common ground with the person we're speaking to. Look for shared interests, experiences, or values that can serve as a foundation for a deeper connection. By building on these similarities, we can create a more meaningful conversation that goes beyond surface-level small talk.

It's also important to give ourselves permission to take breaks when needed. As introverts, we often require time alone to recharge and process our thoughts. If we find ourselves feeling drained during a social interaction, it's okay to step away for a few minutes to regain our energy. Taking care of ourselves in this way allows us to show up fully in our conversations and engage authentically.

Finally, remember that practice makes perfect. Like any skill, the art of conversation requires practice and patience. By intentionally seeking out opportunities for meaningful conversations and actively applying these strategies, we can gradually improve our communication skills and cultivate deeper connections.

Michael, an introverted university student, often felt anxious about participating in class discussions. By setting a goal to contribute one well-thought-out comment or question per class, he gradually built his confidence and became more comfortable sharing his ideas. This practice not only enhanced his learning experience but also led to more engaging conversations with his classmates and professors outside of the classroom.

By embracing these techniques, we can forge stronger bonds with those around us and create a more socially serene and fulfilling life.

So let's dive in and discover the power of conversation together.

Having discussions is crucial for nurturing fulfilling relationships and forming lasting bonds. We excel in conversations that enable connections with others. By understanding our nature, we can focus on quality over quantity in our conversations and emphasize the importance of depth leading to more impactful interactions.

Engaging in conversations involves active listening, where we focus entirely on the speaker, display genuine interest, and respond thoughtfully. It's about being fully present in the discussion and giving our undivided attention to the other person. By actively listening, we are able to grasp subtle hints, comprehend their point of view, and reply with empathy and understanding. This paves the way for deeper and more authentic exchanges to unfold.

When having conversations, it's crucial to ask insightful questions. Rather than asking basic or cliché questions, try delving into more meaningful and thought-provoking inquiries. This demonstrates an interest in understanding the other person and motivates them to reveal more about their thoughts and experiences. By asking insightful questions, we can create a space for more engaging dialogues to take place.

As introverts, we may find it easier to engage in deep conversations simply because we thrive in quieter, more intimate settings. We can leverage this tendency to create an environment that fosters meaningful connections. Instead of seeking out large social gatherings or constantly being in the presence of others, focus on creating opportunities for intimate conversations. Whether it's a one-on-one coffee date or a small group discussion, these settings allow for more authentic and deep conversations to take place.

Quality over quantity in conversation does not mean that we need to have lengthy discussions all the time. It's about the depth of the conversation, not the length. Some of the most profound conversations can be short and to the point. It's about truly connecting with the other person and engaging in meaningful exchange, regardless of the duration. Quantity may give us more interactions, but quality gives us more fulfillment and genuine connections.

By prioritizing quality over quantity in conversation, introverts can forge stronger bonds and cultivate more fulfilling relationships. It allows us to be our authentic selves, connecting on a deeper level with others who appreciate and understand us. So the next time you engage in conversation, remember to actively listen, ask insightful questions, and create opportunities for deep and meaningful connections. This truly is the key to crafting social serenity.

Building strong bonds goes beyond having a social circle. It involves nurturing rewarding relationships based on trust, empathy, and mutual understanding. Let's explore the significance of impactful communications in fostering and sustaining these connections.

Building connections relies heavily on communication. This involves staying true to yourself, openly sharing your thoughts and emotions, and actively listening to others while trying to see things from their point of view. By engaging in transparent conversations, you can cultivate relationships with others, a crucial element in forming strong bonds.

Connection building relies on setting boundaries. Relationships thrive when people respect your preferences and values, and boundaries help make that happen. You may define the type of behavior you expect from others in a relationship and the limits you're willing to tolerate in a relationship by establishing clear boundaries. In addition to ensuring your well-being, this will help you develop a culture of compassion and understanding in your relationships with others.

Active listening is a powerful way to forge strong bonds. When you engage in active listening, you demonstrate to others that you appreciate and honor their thoughts and emotions. This entails focusing on the speaker, seeking clarification through insightful questions, and paraphrasing what has been said. Through actively listening, you can boost your understanding of others and establish a secure and encouraging environment for them to share their thoughts.

Establishing and cultivating connections also requires dedication and commitment. Merely engaging in conversations every now and then is not sufficient. You need to dedicate time and effort to foster your relationships and maintain a connection with those who hold significance in your life. This could entail arranging meet-ups, discovering shared interests to strengthen your bond, or simply reaching out to let someone know they are on your mind. By giving importance to your relationships and actively working on staying connected, you can build strong ties that endure the trials of time.

Picture two introverted friends, Emily and Rachel, who live in different cities. Despite the distance, they make a commitment to nurture their friendship through regular video chats and thoughtful gestures. They take turns initiating conversations, actively listening to each other's concerns, and offering support during challenging times. By consistently investing in their relationship, Emily and Rachel maintain a strong bond that provides a sense of comfort and belonging, even from afar.

To sum it up, forming connections goes beyond having a lot of friends. It involves having meaningful communication, setting personal boundaries, and practicing active listening. By dedicating effort and attention to your relationships, you can build and sustain fulfilling relationships with others. Whether it's with friends, family, or coworkers, keep in mind that strong bonds are rooted in understanding, compassion, and honest dialogue.

Here's a detailed guide:

THE CONVERSATIONAL ROADMAP: A STEP-BY-STEP GUIDE TO DEEPER CONNECTIONS

Step 1: Active Listening and Empathy

- Dedicate your undivided attention to the conversation. Show engagement through eye contact and verbal affirmations.
- Adopt an empathetic approach by striving to understand the speaker's perspective without immediate judgment.

Step 2: Asking Insightful Questions

- Favor open-ended questions to encourage a more detailed response, fostering a conversation that delves deeper.
- Steer clear of yes-or-no questions that tend to stall the conversation.

Step 3: Managing Social Anxiety

- Acknowledge the normalcy of feeling anxious in social settings. Remember, you're not alone in this.
- Before social engagements, practice deep breathing and positive affirmation to mitigate nerves.

Step 4: Setting Conversation Intentions

- Prioritize meaningful dialogue by setting a clear intention before entering social interactions.
- It's perfectly okay to step away and recharge if conversations become overwhelming.

Step 5: Practicing Mindful Listening

- Stay fully engaged in the present conversation, focusing on the speaker's words and body language for cues.
- Genuine interest in the dialogue fosters deeper comprehension and connection.

Step 6: Cultivating Deep Connections

- Shift focus toward nurturing significant relationships that align with your values.
- Dedicate time and effort to understand others while also sharing your authentic self.

Step 7: Setting Personal Boundaries

- Recognize and communicate your own social boundaries to maintain personal well-being.

- Surround yourself with those who respect these boundaries, ensuring a healthy social environment.

Step 8: Practicing Active Listening in Virtual Interactions

- In virtual settings, maintain active listening and empathetic engagement as you would in person.
- Adjusting to the nuances of digital communication retains the depth and authenticity of interactions, despite physical distance.

Embarking on this journey toward crafting social serenity is not just about refining social skills; it's about encompassing the inherent strengths of introversion to build a fulfilling social life. By reshaping how we approach conversations and prioritize relationships, we unlock the door to more meaningful connections. This path not only enriches our social experiences but reflects a more authentic expression of ourselves to the world, creating a ripple effect of positive change. Through this transformative process, we not only discover the joy of deep connections but also the serene confidence in knowing that our social world is one of quality, depth, and meaningful engagement.

Throughout our lives, we engage in countless conversations with others. Some of these interactions are forgettable, mere blips in our memory, while others leave a lasting impact. Have you ever wondered why certain conversations have that power to resonate with us? It's because they go beyond the surface level. They delve deep into our thoughts and emotions, sparking a genuine connection and understanding. As an introvert, you have a natural inclination toward introspection and depth, making you perfectly suited to craft meaningful conversations.

EMBRACE THE POWER OF MEANINGFUL CONNECTIONS

As you navigate the intricate web of social interactions, remember that **quality over quantity** is the golden rule. Truly engaging in conversations with active listening, empathy, and insightful questions can transform your relationships from superficial to profound. By valuing **authentic and genuine interactions**, you pave the way for **stronger connections** built on understanding and empathy.

UPHOLD THE ESSENCE OF AUTHENTIC ENGAGEMENT

In a world where fast-paced exchanges often dominate, prioritize the depth and authenticity of your connections. Nurture relationships that feed your soul, where conversations leave you energized and fulfilled. Remember, it's not about the number of friends but about the quality of those friendships. Stay true to yourself, set personal boundaries, and let your connections flourish through sincerity and active listening.

THE PATH TO SOCIAL FULFILLMENT

As you embark on your journey toward crafting social serenity, carry with you the essence of genuine communication. Cultivate relationships that enrich your life, bring joy to your heart, and support you in times of need. By committing to the art of conversation and fostering strong bonds, you are laying the foundation for a vibrant social life filled with meaningful connections. Trust in the power of positivity and watch how it transforms your world.

NEXT UP

You've mastered the art of crafting social serenity in this chapter. You can navigate social situations with confidence, knowing how to manage your energy and create a social life that respects your introverted needs. But even the most social butterfly needs a place to rest and recharge.

In the following chapter, we'll shift gears to take a look at the cornerstone of introverted well-being: introverted self-care. We'll explore practices that go beyond simply taking breaks. We'll examine strategies for cultivating a deep sense of inner peace and maximizing your introverted recharge.

Imagine returning from social interactions feeling energized, not depleted. Imagine having a wellspring of quiet power within you, ready to be tapped into for creativity, focus, and fulfillment. This chapter equips you with the tools to cultivate that inner sanctuary, a space where you can truly recharge and replenish your introverted spirit.

So take a deep breath and prepare to explore the world of introverted self-care. In the next chapter, we'll guide you on a journey to discover the power of quietude and create a life that allows you to thrive as the introverted powerhouse you are.

CHAPTER 5

RECHARGING
THE QUIET WITHIN

The sunlight filtered through the gauzy curtains with a warm, golden hue, casting a soft glow on the modest collection of potted plants that lined the window sill. Mae stood there, her fingertips grazing the cool glass, feeling the prickle of the morning chill that had yet to give way to the day's warmth. She turned away from the view of the tranquil street below, her small apartment a cocoon of solitude that both comforted and confined.

Inside, Mae found herself wrestling with the low hum of restlessness that often visited on quiet Saturday mornings. It was a familiar intruder, one that reminded her of the delicate balance she sought to maintain as an introvert in a world that shouted where she preferred to whisper. The day loomed ahead, vast and unscheduled—a rare gift and a daunting expanse of time to fill.

The soft shuffle of her feet on the hardwood floor punctuated the silence as she moved through her living space. Everything had its place, an order that seemed to echo the desire for clarity in her mind. Yet as she settled onto the couch, pulling a frayed blanket around her shoulders despite the sun, Mae knew she was skirting the edge of burnout. The week's demands, the conversations that felt like marathons, the perpetual motion—all of it had chipped away at her reserves, leaving her teetering.

A sigh escaped her as she scanned the stack of books on the coffee table, each spine a promise of escape, an affirmation of her need to recharge in quietude. Perhaps today she could dive into the pages, a literary voyage to replenish what the week had drained. Perhaps today she could brush up on her knowledge with a fascinating book, escape into a fictional world to refresh her mind, or connect with herself through the introspection that reading offered.

Mae's eyes then drifted to her small balcony, where a humble chair faced the expanse of city parkland beyond her building. Nature, even in urban vestiges, offered a recalibration of her senses. She imagined the rustling leaves, the chirping of birds, unseen but ever-present, as they orchestrated the symphony of life—a reminder of the world's persistence. She always felt a deep sense of peace in nature and maybe today she could sit amidst nature to renew her spirit, attune to the seasonal shifts and ground herself, or observe the flora and fauna for a serene break.

Friends had invited her out, a well-meaning gesture that should've sparked gratitude, but the thought of social engagement tightened her chest. The comfort of her sanctuary called to her, yet the guilt of declining companionable invitations gnawed at her resolve. Mae knew she must honor her nature, to serenely assert her needs amidst the bustle of a world that rewards social assertiveness. She needed to learn some new skills with confidence such as to politely decline invitations when necessary, offer alternative interactions that aligned with her introverted preferences, or practice articulate self-expression to convey her personal needs with grace.

Boundaries lay at the heart of self-care, tracings in the sand that safeguarded her well-being. They required daily nurturing, an intentionality that Mae knew she must summon even when it felt Herculean. She contemplated the ease with which others set their limits, the way they maneuvered through expectations without faltering. Could she claim that same assertiveness, the gentle firmness to say 'no' and mean it without a tremor of doubt?

The chime of her phone disrupted the quiet, a text from a friend. "Hey, Mae, we're meeting at noon. Can you make it?" Her fingers hovered over the screen, the words forming and dissolving in her mind. How to marry kindness with candor? How to let them see her need for stillness without a trace of offense?

Mae took a breath, then let it out slowly. The reply came, fingertips tapping with careful certainty. "Thank you for the invite, but I'm taking some time for myself today. Let's catch up soon, maybe a quiet dinner next week?"

The phone was set aside, the ripples of her decision spreading, settling, and affirming. She wrapped the comfort of her solitude around her like a shawl. There would be books today, and perhaps a quiet stroll through the park, a nod to the self that thrived on the understated beauty of life. The balance reclaimed, Mae leaned back, a soft smile on her lips as she exhaled a whisper to the stillness: "This is how you survive, isn't it?"

Can we ever truly understand the value of our own solitude, or will it remain an enigma, pressed between the pages of an extroverted tome?

BECOMING YOUR OWN BATTERY CHARGER

Let's face it, the world doesn't run on one energy setting. For introverts venturing through an extrovert-dominated landscape, knowing how to recharge your internal batteries isn't just helpful—it's essential for your well-being. Think of self-care as the power source that fuels your journey through bustling social landscapes and demanding engagements. It's not about isolating yourself but rather ensuring you have the energy to engage in the world on your terms.

One of the most crucial steps may be self-acceptance. **Recognizing and accepting your introversion** as a fundamental part of who you are is essential for authentic self-care. Celebrate your strengths and achievements, and remember, comparing yourself to extroverted norms only detracts from the uniqueness you bring to the table.

Understanding the importance of self-care starts with acknowledging that neglecting it isn't an option if you want to maintain your mental health and avoid the dreaded burnout. Remember, self-care isn't selfish; it's a critical step in making sure you don't end up running on empty. It's about striking a balance that allows you to thrive in both quiet moments alone and while navigating the vibrant chaos of the external world.

Next, **identify personal self-care preferences**. Not all recharge routines are created equal. What brings back your spark? Maybe it's a quiet walk in the park, losing yourself in a book, or engaging in a creative hobby. The key is to listen to your needs and recognize the activities that genuinely refill your energy reserves. Consider keeping a self-care journal as a way to track what works best for you.

Now it's time to **create a recharge routine**. This doesn't have to be a rigid schedule that adds more stress to your life. Instead, think of it as curating a personal collection of energy-boosting activities. Whether it's morning meditation, weekend nature hikes, or simply time spent in solitude, make sure your routine resonates with your personal preferences and fits seamlessly into your lifestyle.

Establishing boundaries is perhaps one of the most crucial steps. It's about saying no to energy-draining activities and yes to what serves your well-being. Clear communication is key here. Setting boundaries is not about pushing people away but about protecting your energy so you can engage with them more fully on your own terms.

Incorporating **daily self-care practices** into your routine ensures that recharging becomes as natural as breathing. Think of it as preventive maintenance for your mental well-being. Small daily actions can accumulate to have a profound effect on your overall energy levels and outlook on life.

Practice mindful self-reflection to tune into your inner needs and desires. This can be through meditation, journaling, or whatever form of reflection resonates with you. It's about making conscious choices that align with your needs, rather than being swept away by the demands of the day.

Lastly, **seek support and accountability**. You don't have to embark on this journey alone. Friends, family, and like-minded communities can offer encouragement and remind you of the importance of your self-care practice, especially on days when it feels particularly challenging to prioritize your needs. Now let's recap:

THE PATH TO EMPOWERED RECHARGING

Self-care for introverts isn't about following a fad or chasing fleeting trends. It's about recognizing a fundamental need for activities that replenish your energy and create a life that feels sustainable and fulfilling. Here's a roadmap to guide you on your empowered recharging journey:

1. **Understand the Importance of Self-Care: Acknowledge Self-Care as a Necessity, Not a Luxury.** Think of yourself as a high-performance device. Just like your phone needs regular charging to function optimally, you too need dedicated time for self-care to avoid burnout. Ignoring this need can lead to feelings of exhaustion, irritability, and

difficulty concentrating. Imagine the impact this could have on your work, relationships, and overall well-being.

2. **Identify Personal Self-Care Preferences: Reflect on Activities that Replenish Your Energy.** This isn't a one-size-fits-all approach. What energizes one introvert might drain another. *J.K. Rowling, the author of Harry Potter, finds solace in long walks—a perfect opportunity to unwind, clear her head, and spark creativity.* Perhaps for you, it's curling up with a good book and a cup of tea or spending a quiet afternoon tinkering in your garden. Pay attention to how you feel after engaging in different activities. Notice which ones leave you feeling refreshed and recharged, ready to tackle the world again.

3. **Create a Recharge Routine: Curate a Collection of Personal Energy-Boosting Activities.** Now that you know what activities replenish your energy, weave them into the fabric of your life. Schedule dedicated "me-time" in your calendar, just like you would an important meeting. This could be a relaxing bath before bed, an afternoon spent listening to calming music and journaling, or a solo hike in nature. *Albert Einstein, a renowned physicist and a self-proclaimed introvert, valued his time alone for deep thinking and theorizing.* Perhaps you can emulate his approach and dedicate specific times for focused work and reflection.

4. **Establish Boundaries: Protect Your Time and Energy by Communicating Your Needs.** Being introverted doesn't mean being antisocial. However, you have the right to manage your social interactions in a way that feels comfortable for you. Communicate your need for alone time openly and honestly with friends, family, and colleagues. Explain that after social gatherings, you might need some quiet time to recharge. A simple "I had a wonderful time, but I need a quiet evening to myself to

feel re-energized" can go a long way in setting healthy boundaries.

5. **Prioritize Daily Self-Care Practices: Incorporate Small, Beneficial Actions into Your Daily Routine.** Self-care doesn't have to be a grand gesture. Small daily acts can make a big difference. Start your day with a few minutes of mindful breathing or meditation. Enjoy a healthy breakfast that fuels your body and mind. Take short breaks throughout the workday to stretch, walk outside, or simply close your eyes and take a few deep breaths. These small acts accumulate, creating a foundation of well-being throughout the day.

6. **Practice Mindful Self-Reflection: Connect with Your Inner Needs Through Reflection.** Schedule regular time for introspection. Journal about your experiences, identify areas where you might be neglecting your needs, and celebrate your self-care victories. Ask yourself questions like: "What activities leave me feeling energized?" or "What situations drain my energy the most?" By becoming more aware of your internal cues, you can make adjustments to your life and create a more supportive environment for your introverted nature.

7. **Seek Support and Accountability: Lean on a Community or Loved Ones to Keep You Focused on Your Self-Care Journey.** Surround yourself with supportive people who understand and respect your need for solitude. Join introverted online communities or find a friend who shares your introverted nature. Having a network of support can help you stay motivated on your self-care journey. They can be your cheerleaders, offering encouragement and celebrating your successes.

8. **Adjust and Adapt: Be Open to Changing Your Routine as Your Needs Evolve.** Life is dynamic, and your needs might change over time. Perhaps a recharge routine that

worked well for you in your twenties no longer serves you in your thirties. Be open to adapting your self-care practices as your life circumstances evolve. The key is to remain mindful of your introverted needs and adjust your approach accordingly.

Each step is designed to help you maintain a balanced and healthy life by honoring your introverted nature. Through these practices, you're not just surviving in a world geared toward extroverted individuals; you're thriving with confidence and authenticity.

Self-care is not an extravagance but a requirement for introverts to maintain their mental well-being and avoid burnout. As an introvert, you may have experienced the draining effects of constantly navigating a culture that values gregariousness. The noise, the crowds, the small talk—it can all be overwhelming and exhausting. But by prioritizing activities that replenish your energy, you can protect your mental health and find balance in a world that often feels off-kilter.

One of the first steps in practicing self-care as an introvert is to enhance your self-awareness around your introverted qualities and preferences. Understand that it is perfectly okay to need alone time to recharge, and that your energy comes from within. Recognize that you thrive in quieter, more reflective environments, and that socializing may take more of a toll on you. This self-awareness will allow you to make informed choices about how and when to engage with others and when to prioritize time for yourself.

Self-care is crucial for introverts because it helps them avoid burnout and maintain positive mental well-being. When introverts push themselves too hard or try to fit into extroverted patterns, they can become overwhelmed and exhausted. Taking time for self-care allows introverts to recharge their energy and prevent these negative effects from taking hold.

Practicing self-care as an introvert means being intentional about setting boundaries and honoring your introverted nature. It means giving yourself permission to say "no" to social engagements that drain you, instead prioritizing activities that bring you joy and replenish your energy. It means creating a routine that allows for ample alone time and solitude, where you can engage in activities that nourish your soul, such as reading a book, listening to music, or pursuing a hobby.

Setting boundaries is an essential part of self-care for introverts. It means communicating your needs and limits to others and advocating for yourself. It means protecting your time and energy by saying "no" to things that do not align with your values or priorities. By setting boundaries, introverts can create a safe space for themselves to recharge and avoid the feelings of overwhelm and exhaustion that can come from constantly being pulled in different directions.

It's important for introverts to prioritize self-care, which isn't selfish but an act of self-preservation. By looking after yourself and embracing your tendencies, you can present yourself to the world. This allows you to confidently maneuver through a society that typically favors extroverts, all while having the tools and techniques to safeguard your health.

As you start your path to self-care as an introvert, focus on activities that recharge your energy, set boundaries to safeguard your time and health, and honor your introverted nature. This approach can lead to a nourishing and well-rounded life, allowing you to flourish authentically as an introvert, in a world that often celebrates extroverted traits.

One of the first steps in creating a recharge routine is embracing self-acceptance. It's crucial to welcome your traits and acknowledge that it's okay to prioritize your own needs for alone time and contemplation. Society often places emphasis on extroversion, but introverts possess strengths and viewpoints that deserve appreciation. By accepting yourself and respecting your own needs, you can kick-start the process of fostering a profound understanding of yourself and self-value.

Earlier, we discussed the importance of identifying activities that replenish your energy. This is an ongoing process, and keeping a self-care inventory can be helpful. Regularly revisit this list and adjust it as your needs or preferences change. For introverts, activities that replenish energy often means seeking out quiet and solitary experiences. Spending time in nature can be incredibly therapeutic and rejuvenating for introverts, as it provides an opportunity to escape the noise and chaos of the world and reconnect with your own inner quiet. Whether it's a walk in the park, a hike in the woods, or simply sitting by a tranquil lake, nature has a way of soothing the introverted soul.

Solitude is another essential component of a recharge routine for introverts. Carving out time for yourself, free from distractions and external demands, allows you to recharge your energy and process your thoughts and emotions. Whether it's reading a book, taking a long bath, or simply sitting in silence, finding moments of solitude can be deeply nourishing for introverts.

Indulging in hobbies that bring you happiness and satisfaction is also a vital part of a recharge routine. Whether it's painting, playing a musical instrument, gardening, or engaging in any pastime that ignites your passion, pursuing these interests enables you to unleash your creativity and rejuvenate your spirit. These hobbies offer a sense of fulfillment and meaning that can deeply influence your sense of wellness.

In addition to these activities, it's important to maintain balance by setting healthy boundaries that safeguard your self-care and well-being. This means saying no to social engagements when you need time to recharge and allocating dedicated periods in your agenda for personal reflection and quiet time. By respecting your need for solitude and establishing boundaries, you can guarantee that you prioritize taking care of yourself.

As we've discussed, creating a recharge routine is essential for introverts to maintain their mental well-being and avoid burnout. By prioritizing activities that replenish your energy, such as spending time in nature, solitude, and pursuing hobbies, you can navigate the demands of a culture that prizes external stimulation with quiet strength. Keep in mind, self-care is not a luxury but a necessity for introverts, and by setting boundaries and honoring your introverted nature, you can create a healthier and more balanced life. Following is a recap of the strategies to support your recharge routine.

SETTING BOUNDARIES: NURTURING YOUR INTROVERTED NATURE

As an introvert, you possess a natural inclination to protect your energy and prioritize self-care. However, in a rushed society that often values constant activity and social interaction, setting boundaries becomes crucial for maintaining your mental well-being and cultivating a balanced life. Establishing healthy boundaries allows you to honor and nurture your introverted nature, creating the space and time you need to recharge and rejuvenate.

1. Recognize the Importance of Boundaries

Boundaries serve as guidelines, not walls to shut others out. They help cultivate self-respect and guarantee that your own needs are taken care of. By setting boundaries, you are allowed to communicate your limits and grant yourself the freedom to safeguard your time and energy. Recognize that prioritizing your well-being is not selfish; it is an act of self-care that empowers you to show up as your best self in every aspect of your life.

2. Tune in to Your Inner Compass

To set effective boundaries, you must first become aware of your own needs and limitations. Take the time to reflect on what drains you and what replenishes you. Notice the situations, environments, and people that energize or deplete you. Pay attention to your internal cues and emotions, and use them as guidance to create boundaries that support your introverted nature.

3. Learn to Say No

One of the most empowering ways to set boundaries is by learning to say no without guilt or apology. Understand that saying no is not a rejection of others; it is a respectful acknowledgment of your own needs. Practice assertiveness and communicate your limits clearly and kindly. Remember, you have the right to decline invitations or requests that do not align with your priorities or drain your energy.

4. Protect Your Sacred Self-Care Time

Make self-care a must-do in your routine by setting aside dedicated time for activities that recharge you. Whether it's diving into a book, taking a stroll in nature, or pampering yourself with a soothing bath, prioritize these moments for your overall health. Let those close to you know that this time is crucial, and defend it with determination. By valuing your self-care routine, you not only cater to your own needs but also demonstrate to others around you that your boundaries are important.

5. Communicate Clearly and Kindly

Effectively setting boundaries requires clear and open communication. Be upfront and transparent with others about your needs and limitations. Use "I" statements to express yourself and avoid blaming or shaming others. Practice active listening and validate others' feelings while also maintaining firm boundaries. Strive for a harmonious balance between assertiveness and empathy in your interactions.

6. Surround Yourself with Supportive Relationships

Connect with people who respect and appreciate your introverted tendencies. Surround yourself with individuals who understand and cherish your desire for solitude, peace, and self-care. Look for individuals and groups where you can feel valued and acknowledged. Creating a circle of relationships will not just give you a feeling of acceptance but also strengthen your dedication to setting personal boundaries.

7. Review and Reflect Regularly

Setting boundaries is an ongoing task that requires introspection and adaptability. Take the time to evaluate and contemplate your boundaries regularly. Check if they still match your requirements and situation. Make adjustments as needed to guarantee they remain effective in safeguarding and promoting your wellness.

Always remember that setting boundaries is a way to show yourself love and care. When you create boundaries, you're safeguarding your time, energy, and overall wellness. Recognize your introverted nature and respect your needs. This allows you to create a space for self-care and replenishment, leading to a life that's more balanced, joyful, and fulfilling in the long run.

EMBRACING BALANCE FOR A FULFILLING LIFE

In the hustle and bustle of our daily lives, finding **time for self-care** often takes a back seat. However, for introverts navigating an environment that undervalues solitude and introspection, it is not just a lavish treat but is essential to safeguarding their mental well-being. By embracing self-awareness and understanding their unique qualities and preferences, introverts can create a life that fuels rather than drains them.

ESTABLISHING HEALTHY BOUNDARIES: REAL-LIFE EXAMPLES

Social Invitations: Instead of just saying "no" to social engagements, provide examples like:

- "Thank you for the invite! I'd love to catch up, but this weekend is already quite packed. Maybe we can plan a quieter get-together next week?"
- "I know you love group outings, but large gatherings can be draining for me. Would you be interested in a one-on-one coffee date sometime?"

Phone Calls/Texts:

- "I appreciate the call, but I'm in the middle of something quiet right now. Can I return your call a little later?" (Follow up with a specific timeframe.)
- "Texting works best for me most of the time. Feel free to reach out that way if you need something."

Work-Life Balance:

- "I value my evenings for decompression. Can urgent requests wait until tomorrow morning?"
- "While I'm happy to help, completing this task by the end of the day would require me to work through my usual break time. Would offering it by tomorrow be an option?"

NEXT UP

Ah, the quiet hum of contentment. You've journeyed through the art of introverted self-care in this chapter. You've built a haven within yourself, a sanctuary where your introverted spirit can flourish.

Now, with your wellspring of introverted energy replenished, it's time to step out—but not without your power source.

In the next chapter, we'll embark on a transformative journey of reframing. We'll leave behind the misconceptions and societal pressures that often paint introversion as a limitation. We'll delve into the unique strengths that lie at the core of your introverted nature and explore how to leverage them to achieve success and fulfillment on your own terms.

Imagine this: a world where your introverted nature isn't a secret to be hidden but a badge of honor to be worn proudly. Imagine transforming the quiet power you've cultivated into your superpower, a force that allows you to excel in ways that resonate with your deepest needs. This chapter equips you with the tools to rewrite the narrative and redefine what it means to thrive as an introvert.

So shed any lingering doubts and get ready to take in the power of quietude. In the upcoming chapter, we'll guide you on a path to introverted liberation, empowering you to claim your space in the world and shine brightly, positively, authentically, and powerfully. After all, the world needs the unique perspective and strengths that only introverts can offer. Let's rewrite the script and show the world the true potential that lies within the quiet.

CHAPTER 6

FROM LIMITATIONS TO LIBERATION

In the dim light of early morning, Eva sat on the edge of her bed, the corners of the room still clinging to the night's shadow. The quiet was a canvas, and her mind painted thoughts with broad strokes. She had always known the comfort of silence, a landscape for reflection where she could dance with her thoughts un-criticized. Yet within the quiet, a recurring echo of doubt whispered, and she strained to silence it. When confronting the throbbing heart of her own business, her resolve wavered, a creek threatening to become a chasm.

With a cup of hot coffee in hand, Eva paced her small apartment, which doubled as her workspace. Shelves lined with books on entrepreneurship and personal development mirrored her aspirations, but the ghost of a belief whispered that she was not cut from the same cloth as those who so confidently mapped their way to success. Could she, an introvert in an extrovert world, harness her potential or would her inner critic win?

On the street below, car engines growled to life, and she watched as people moved with purpose. They possessed an air of assurance that seemed foreign to her. Yet wasn't growth a field lying fallow in everyone until the seeds of effort sprouted? She recalled reading that "talent is nurtured, not born," and the idea sat in her palm like a pebble, smooth and real. She turned it over and over, finding comfort in its weight.

Afternoon light sifted through the blinds, cutting sharp lines across the hardwood floor. She sat at the desk, papers strewn about like leaves in autumn, each leaf an idea, a vision, a fragment of a dream. And with every decision to embrace a new challenge, the weight of uncertainty pressed against her chest. But isn't this the forge where mental fortitude is tempered, where challenges are the anvil and determination the hammer?

In moments when the shadows of doubt loomed, Eva reached for her journal, her reservoir of past setbacks and triumphant rebounds. Every entry was a testament to her perseverance. The smell of ink and paper was a reminder of the tangibility of her journey. And as the sun dipped below the horizon, painting the sky with strokes of fire and melancholy, she pondered a life wherein challenges were but stepping stones, leading her to vistas yet unseen. Could it be that the stories we ink for ourselves are the chapters we never knew we could write?

BREAKING THE CHAINS OF LIMITING BELIEFS

You know those thoughts that hold you back? The ones that say, 'You can't do this' or 'You're not good enough'? Those are your limiting beliefs. They're like an invisible fence keeping you from reaching your full potential, and the worst part is, you might not even realize they're there. For introverts, especially in a world that seemingly rewards extroversion, these barriers can appear insurmountable. Yet, it's crucial to understand that **the real battle is waged within the mind.** Acknowledging and challenging these self-imposed constraints is the first step toward achieving a brighter, opportunity-filled future.

At the heart of this journey is the transition from a fixed mindset, which dictates that our abilities and potential are static, to a growth mindset, which opens us up to a world of endless possibilities. This mindset shift is not just beneficial; it's essential for anyone aiming to overcome personal and professional barriers. It allows us to view challenges not as dead-ends but as stepping stones on the path to growth and development.

CULTIVATING A GROWTH MINDSET

Cultivating a growth mindset starts with recognizing that every skill is learnable, and every challenge is an opportunity to expand our capabilities. This doesn't mean that the journey will be easy. On the contrary, it will be filled with trials and setbacks. But it's in facing these challenges head-on that we find our true strength. **Resilience is built in the crucible of adversity.**

For introverts, this might mean stepping out of comfort zones and embracing situations that demand communication and assertiveness. It could involve speaking up in meetings, networking despite internal resistance, or even taking on leadership positions. These actions don't just build skills; they shatter the glass ceiling of limiting beliefs.

REAL STORIES, REAL GROWTH

Let me share a story. Mark, an introvert by nature, always believed he was destined to remain in the background. Leadership and public speaking were, in his mind, reserved for the naturally outgoing. Yet when faced with a project that no one else would champion, Mark stepped up. Despite initial hiccups and overwhelming anxiety, he persevered. The project was not just a success; it became a turning point in his career. **Mark's story is a testament to the power of challenging limiting beliefs and seizing growth opportunities.**

EMBRACING CHALLENGES AS OPPORTUNITIES

The essence of positive thinking lies in seeing every hurdle not as a stop sign but as a signpost, guiding us toward growth and development. This perspective is especially powerful for introverts in a world that favors the bold and the brave. It's about leveraging your unique strengths, such as deep thinking, empathy, and the ability to listen, and turning them into powerful tools in both personal and professional realms.

To this end, **embracing challenges as opportunities** is not just about facing fear; it's about redefining fear. It's about shifting the narrative from "I can't because I'm an introvert" to "I can, and being an introvert gives me a unique advantage."

- **Identify the limiting belief:** Acknowledge the thought holding you back. It could be 'I'm not good at public speaking' or 'I can never be a leader because I'm too reserved.'
- **Challenge it:** Ask yourself, is this belief based on fact or just your perception? Look for evidence that contradicts this belief.
- **Replace it:** Swap the limiting belief with a growth-oriented one. Instead of 'I'm not good at public speaking,' try 'I can develop my public speaking skills with practice.'

STRATEGIES FOR DEVELOPMENT AND GROWTH

For introverts looking to develop resilience, bounce back from setbacks, and maintain optimism, consider the following strategies:

- **Lean into your strengths:** Introversion brings gifts like thoughtful analysis and deep focus. Use these to your advantage.
- **Practice self-compassion:** Learning and growth involve setbacks. Be kind to yourself during the process.

- **Seek small wins:** Growth is cumulative. Celebrate the small victories along the way; they add up to significant progress.
- **Surround yourself with support:** A network of encouragement can make all the difference. Find mentors, friends, or colleagues who uplift you.

In a world that often feels designed for the extrovert, finding your place as an introvert isn't just about adapting; it's about flourishing. By challenging limiting beliefs and cultivating a growth mindset, you're not just surviving; you're thriving. It's a journey of transformation, from limitations to liberation, and it starts with a single step: believing in the power of positive thinking.

Identifying and challenging limiting beliefs is a crucial step toward personal and professional growth. These beliefs can hold us back, preventing us from reaching our full potential and living the life we truly desire. They serve as self-imposed barriers, dictating what we believe is possible for ourselves and what we can achieve.

Limiting beliefs are often formed early in life, influenced by societal norms, cultural expectations, and past experiences. They can manifest as negative thoughts or self-doubt, such as "I'm not good enough," "I don't have what it takes," or "I'll never succeed." These beliefs create a fixed mindset, where we perceive our abilities as fixed traits and are resistant to change.

To challenge these beliefs, we first need to become aware of them. Pay attention to the negative thoughts and self-talk that come up when you confront challenges or consider stepping outside of your comfort zone. Recognize that these beliefs are not facts but rather subjective interpretations of your abilities and potential.

Next, question the validity of these beliefs. Ask yourself if there is any evidence to support them. Are they based on past failures or rejection? Are they influenced by the opinions of others?

Challenge these beliefs by seeking alternative perspectives and reframing your thoughts.

For example, if you believe you're not good at public speaking, question why you hold this belief. Is it because you had a negative experience in the past? Instead of seeing that experience as a reflection of your abilities, consider it as an opportunity for growth. Recognize that public speaking is a skill that can be developed with practice and learning.

Another powerful strategy is to seek evidence to disprove your limiting beliefs. Look for examples of people who have succeeded despite facing similar challenges or adversity. Surround yourself with positive role models and seek their guidance or mentorship. By seeing others who have overcome their own limitations, you'll begin to realize that your own barriers are not insurmountable.

Finally, replace your limiting beliefs with empowering ones. Choose affirmations and positive statements that support your growth and development. Focus on your strengths and accomplishments, and remind yourself of the progress you've already made. By cultivating a growth mindset and embracing the possibilities for growth and change, you'll begin to see yourself and your potential in a new light. In reality, limiting beliefs are often tied to a fixed mindset. Let's look at some strategies for challenging your limiting beliefs.

CHALLENGE YOUR LIMITING BELIEFS AND UNLEASH YOUR TRUE POTENTIAL

By identifying and challenging your limiting beliefs, you can break free from the constraints that have been holding you back. Grab the possibilities for growth and change and recognize that your potential is not defined by your past or your current circumstances. With a growth mindset and a willingness to step outside of your comfort zone, you can achieve greatness and create a life that aligns with your true desires and aspirations.

Imagine if you approached every obstacle, setback, or limitation with a mindset that sees it as an opportunity for growth and learning. By cultivating a growth mindset, you can transform your perspective and unlock your true potential. Instead of being paralyzed by self-doubt or discouraged by challenges, you can elevate them as valuable stepping stones on your journey to success.

A growth mindset is a belief that your abilities and intelligence can be developed through dedication, effort, and perseverance. It is the understanding that failure and setbacks are not permanent but rather temporary setbacks that can be overcome with the right mindset and strategies. When you have a growth mindset, you view challenges as opportunities to learn and grow, and you believe that your abilities are not fixed but can be improved over time.

To cultivate a growth mindset, you must first become aware of any limiting beliefs that may be holding you back. These beliefs are often deeply ingrained and can shape your thoughts, actions, and behaviors. They may include beliefs such as 'I'm not smart enough,' 'I'll never be good at this,' or 'I'm not worthy of success.' By identifying these beliefs and challenging their validity, you can start to replace them with more empowering and positive beliefs.

One effective way to challenge limiting beliefs is through self-reflection and questioning. Ask yourself why you hold these beliefs and whether there is any evidence to support them. Often, you will find that these beliefs are based on assumptions or past experiences that may no longer be true or relevant. As was discussed more in depth in Chapter 2: replace negative thoughts with positive affirmations and reminders of your past successes and strengths to reinforce a growth mindset.

It is also important to surround yourself with a positive and supportive environment. Seek out individuals who have a growth mindset and who can inspire and motivate you on your journey. Engage in activities that challenge you and provide opportunities for growth and development. By immersing yourself in an environment that promotes personal growth and resilience, you can strengthen your mindset and overcome personal and professional barriers.

In addition to challenging limiting beliefs, it is crucial to adopt a proactive approach to learning and development. Be excited for new experiences, seek out feedback, and view failures as valuable lessons. Shift your focus from the outcome to the process, and celebrate progress and effort rather than just the end result. By reframing your mindset in this way, you can develop resilience, adaptability, and a willingness to take on new challenges.

Remember, cultivating a growth mindset is an ongoing process. It requires consistent effort, self-reflection, and a commitment to personal growth. But with a growth mindset, you can overcome personal and professional barriers and thrive in a society that often caters to extroverted qualities. Embrace challenges, view setbacks as opportunities for growth, and believe in your ability to learn and adapt. With a growth mindset, you have the power to transform your life and achieve your true potential.

Life presents obstacles, from small inconveniences to major hurdles Introverts, in particular, may find these challenges overwhelming due to their preference for steering clear of conflicts or discomfort. However, seeing setbacks as opportunities can lead to personal and professional growth, enhanced mental resilience, and a more positive perspective on life.

1. **Change your perspective**: Instead of viewing challenges as problems to solve, try reframing them as opportunities for development. Each challenge brings with it the chance

to learn something new, hone abilities, and gather useful experiences. By changing your viewpoint, you can tackle challenges with a spirit of curiosity and enthusiasm rather than being overwhelmed by fear and worry.

2. **Embrace discomfort**: Venturing outside of our comfort zones often leads to personal and professional growth. When we explore new territories, we push ourselves to gain knowledge and skills that we might not have previously thought possible. Embracing discomfort is essential for our growth, helping us expand our perspectives and unlock our potential.

3. **Practice resilience**: Being resilient means being able to overcome obstacles and tough times. It is a crucial skill for dealing with life's ups and downs and maintaining a positive outlook. One effective way to build resilience is by facing challenges with a mindset of learning and development. Rather than seeing setbacks as failures, consider them as chances to grow and improve.

4. **Cultivate optimism**: Having an optimistic mindset is key when facing difficulties. By staying positive and having faith in your ability to conquer hurdles, you can boost your likelihood of achieving your goals. Fostering optimism involves expressing gratitude, surrounding yourself with positive people, and countering any negative self-talk.

5. **Develop a growth mindset**: Having a growth mindset means believing that with effort and determination, you can enhance your abilities and intelligence. Viewing challenges as opportunities for learning and growth is an aspect of this mindset. It enables you to see setbacks as temporary rather than reflections of your skills.

6. **Seek support**: Remember, you don't have to tackle difficulties alone. Reach out to your loved ones, friends, or a mentor for support and guidance. Opening up about your challenges with others allows you to see things from

different angles and gather advice that could assist you in conquering hurdles with greater ease.

7. **Take small steps**: Breaking down challenges into smaller, more achievable tasks can help reduce their overwhelming nature. By making progress toward your objectives, you can build your self-assurance and momentum. Rejoice in every accomplishment during the journey, and be open to modifying your path as necessary.

By embracing challenges as opportunities for growth and development, introverts can build mental fortitude, resilience, and optimism. By shifting your mindset, accepting discomfort, and seeking support, you can navigate challenges with confidence and come out stronger on the other side. Remember, challenges are not meant to hold you back but to propel you forward on your personal and professional journey.

EMBRACING YOUR JOURNEY TO GROWTH

As you reflect back on the journey you've taken to challenge your limiting beliefs, cultivate a growth mindset, and take in challenges as stepping stones to development, remember that this transformation is a continuous process. **Identifying and challenging limiting beliefs** is not a one-time task but an ongoing commitment to self-discovery and personal growth. By continuously questioning the beliefs that hold you back, you create space for new possibilities and opportunities to unfold.

Cultivating a growth mindset is a powerful tool that can help you navigate personal and professional barriers with resilience and determination. As you face challenges, remember that setbacks are not the end of the road but valuable lessons that propel you forward. Own a mindset of growth, viewing obstacles as opportunities to learn, adapt, and grow stronger.

Embracing challenges as opportunities for development is a mindset shift that can lead to enhanced mental fortitude, resilience, and optimism. Each challenge you encounter is a chance to build your capacity to bounce back, learn from adversity, and emerge stronger than before. By viewing challenges as essential components of your growth journey, you empower yourself to excel in an extroverted society as an introvert.

MOVING FORWARD WITH OPTIMISM AND COURAGE

Keep in mind that as you progress in your personal and professional development, your path will be special and significant. Each effort you make to surpass obstacles and tackle challenges showcases your strength and ability to bounce back. **Celebrate your progress**, no matter how small, using each lesson learned as a stepping stone for what lies ahead.

Stay committed to your growth by approaching each new challenge with an open attitude and a desire to gain knowledge. Encompass uncertainties with courage and positivity, understanding that every hurdle you encounter is a chance for growth and exploration. Your resilience and optimism have no bounds. As you overcome each challenge, you enhance your capacity to succeed in a world that can sometimes seem daunting.

Believe in your ability to rise above any challenge that comes your way. Rely on your inner strength and persistence to confront challenges directly, knowing that every triumph propels you toward your goals. Greet each new day with eagerness and curiosity, as the opportunities for progress and advancement are endless when you welcome them with sincerity and a positive mindset.

A BRIGHT FUTURE AWAITS

As you close this chapter of your growth journey, don't forget that the strength to overcome obstacles and thrive in a society that may not always appreciate your talent resides within you. By questioning your beliefs, nurturing a growth mindset, and viewing challenges as opportunities for growth, you have armed yourself with the tools to shape a future brimming with accomplishments, contentment, and resilience. **You are capable of achieving great things**, and your journey to freedom is just starting. Keep pushing forward with optimism, bravery, and faith in your own capabilities. The world eagerly anticipates seeing you radiate in all your brilliance.

NEXT UP

Now that you've started on this part of the journey of breaking from limiting beliefs and embracing a growth mindset, it's time to focus on the future. In Chapter 7: Envisioning Your Introverted Success, we'll discuss ways to create a vision for your life, one that emphasizes your strengths and preferences as an introvert. We'll look into strategies for setting goals that resonate with your values and dreams and explore methods for overcoming challenges and achieving long-lasting success. This is your chance to vividly imagine what fulfillment means to you and map out a plan to reach it. Are you ready to step into your introverted power and shape a life that propels your success and sparks your interests?

CHAPTER 7

ENVISIONING YOUR INTROVERTED SUCCESS

The morning sun filtered through the mist, casting a soft glow over the small seaside town where Emma lived. She stood at the shoreline, the cold surf washing over her bare feet and the cries of gulls merging with the rhythm of the waves. Each ebb and flow carried the whispers of introspection, beckoning her to redefine the success that had always seemed a distant marker set by an unforgiving society.

Emma closed her eyes, letting the salt-scented breeze tease her hair. She conjured an image of the bookstore she longed to own, its shelves a place for minds that craved the comfort of quietude. Visualization, she knew, was power; the power to craft a world where her introversion was not a hindrance but her guiding force.

She imagined the bell above the door tinkling as a customer entered, the soft murmur of pages turning, the cozy nooks that invited one to sit and stay. But a vision alone was like a ship without a rudder, and Emma understood the need for a map to guide her journey. With the clarity of intention, she began to outline her goals, adhering to the SMART framework that would become her compass:

- **Specific**: Open a bookstore that catered to introverts, offering a calm space for reading and reflection.
- **Measurable**: Secure a lending institution's approval for a business loan within the next six months.
- **Achievable**: Research successful bookstore models and draft a business plan within three months.
- **Relevant**: Curate a selection of books that resonated with her and would likely appeal to like-minded patrons.
- **Time-bound**: Launch the bookstore no later than eighteen months from now.

As she sketched these thoughts in the damp sand, the urgency of her dream impressed upon her the transience of time. Her pulse quickened with the tide's retreat, and she felt the pressing need to act. Yet the world moved swiftly around her, too often discounting the quiet fortitude of the soul that thrived in solitude.

The clang of a distant buoy called her back to the present. A child ran past, his laughter cutting through the solitude of the morning, reminding her that life's fabric was woven from a multitude of threads, each significant in its pattern. Success, she mused, was not a loud proclamation but a personal testament, written in the silent language of persistence and peace.

Emma returned home to walls lined with books, each spine a friend that spoke in hushed tones of the distance between dreams and reality. Her journal lay open on the table, its pages awaiting the blueprint of a life reimagined. Yet amidst the planning and dreaming lay an inherent question that brushed against her consciousness like a leaf in the wind:

What if the quiet power of reflection and the courage to define one's own path could indeed shape a future where contentment and success were not strangers but companions in the dance of life?

FROM INNER REFLECTIONS TO OUTER SUCCESS

Success might just be one of the most overused and underexplored terms in our vocabulary today. Everywhere we turn, society throws at us images of what it means to be successful: high-powered jobs, extravagant lifestyles, and endless social events. But here's a thought: What if success isn't one-size-fits-all, especially for the introverts among us? This is where the power of positive thinking comes into play, not just as a fleeting idea but as a transformative practice for introverts striving to define success on their own terms.

For too long, the introverted person has been misunderstood, seen through the lens of what they're not rather than celebrated for what they are. It's high time we flip the script. Success, particularly for someone who thrives in introspection and deep thought, should be a personal ode to their unique strengths and visions. It's about **finding fulfillment and achievement in ways that resonate with you**, not chasing after a societal checklist of what you should have or should be doing.

As an introvert, Satya Nadella, the CEO of Microsoft, redefined success not just through financial metrics but by creating a more empathetic and inclusive culture at Microsoft. Under his leadership, the company has embraced a "growth mindset" that values collaboration and continuous learning over individual achievement.

Redefining Success is our first port of call. Let's challenge the mainstream narrative together. Success for an introvert can mean having the space and time for deep work without the constant interruption of an open office space. It might be building meaningful, one-on-one relationships rather than amassing a huge network of acquaintances. The point is, your definition of success should empower you and reflect your core values and interests.

Next, we delve into **The Power of Visualization**. Visualization isn't just daydreaming about your ideal future; it's a potent tool for setting your subconscious to work on your goals. For introverts, this practice can be particularly powerful. It's a chance to quiet the external noise and deeply connect with your aspirations. Through visualization, you can construct a vivid, positive vision of your future where your introverted strengths shine. This vision can guide your actions and decision-making, aligning them with your personal definition of success.

Lastly, **setting SMART Goals** is about making your vision actionable. Sure, it's great to have a dream, but how do you get there? This is where specific, measurable, achievable, relevant, and time-bound goals come into play. By setting SMART goals, you create a roadmap to your vision of success. Each goal acts like a stepping stone, breaking down the journey into manageable, concrete steps. Whether it's enhancing your skills, building deeper connections, or creating work that resonates with your values, SMART goals help you focus your efforts where they matter most.

Imagine redefining success in a way that truly reflects who you are. Consider the energy and motivation that springs from pursuing goals aligned with your personal aspirations. By harnessing the power of positive thinking, introverts can carve out a path to success that's not only fulfilling but also authentic to their nature.

I'll share stories of introverts who've walked this path, turning inward to understand their deepest desires and outward to achieve their unique vision of success. Through their journeys, we'll see the incredible potential that lies in embracing our introverted selves and thinking positively about our capabilities and futures.

So are you ready to envision your introverted success and make it a reality? Let's challenge the norms, embrace our strengths, and celebrate the achievement of success on our terms. It's not just about flourishing in the over-stimulated world of extroverts; it's about redefining what success means for you and how you can achieve it while staying true to your introverted self.

The first step in redefining success is to let go of societal expectations and the pressure to conform. As an introvert, you may have different priorities and values than those around you, and that's okay. Success shouldn't be about meeting someone else's definition; it should be about living a life that aligns with your authentic self.

To begin this process, take some time to reflect on what success means to you. Consider your passions, values, and what truly brings you fulfillment. It could be anything from making a positive impact on others to pursuing a career that aligns with your interests and strengths. Don't limit yourself to what society tells you success should look like. Remember, success is a deeply personal and individual concept.

Once you've identified what success means to you, it's important to create a clear vision for your future. Visualization can be a powerful tool for introverts to create a positive mental image of the success they desire. Take a few moments each day to envision yourself achieving your goals, living the life you've defined as success. See yourself thriving in your career, building meaningful relationships, and finding fulfillment in all areas of your life.

But creating a vision is just the first step. To turn that vision into reality, you need to set goals that align with it. This is where the SMART goal framework comes in. By setting goals that meet the SMART criteria, you can break your vision down into actionable steps and track your progress along the way.

Remember, success is not a one-size-fits-all concept. It's about defining what it means to you and taking meaningful steps toward achieving it. Celebrate your introversion, honor your values, and envision a future that aligns with your authentic self. When you do, you'll find a sense of fulfillment and authenticity in your achievements that cannot be measured by societal standards.

Embracing your unique definition of success is the first step toward a fulfilling life as an introvert. But how do you go about visualizing your ideal future? Let's explore the power of visualization in the next section.

Visualization is a powerful tool that can help introverts create a clear and positive vision for their future. By mentally imagining themselves achieving their goals and living their desired life, introverts can tap into their innate strengths and motivations. Visualization allows introverts to focus their energy, clarify their goals, and increase their confidence in their abilities. It also helps introverts overcome obstacles and setbacks, as they can envision themselves finding solutions and moving forward.

As a quiet thinker, Katharine L'Heureux, introverted founder of Kahina Giving Beauty, visualized creating a socially conscious beauty brand that empowers women and supports communities in Morocco. Through vivid visualization and aligning her actions with her vision, she made her dream a reality.

To begin using visualization as a tool for success, introverts can start by finding a quiet and comfortable space where they can relax and focus. They can close their eyes and take a few deep breaths to calm their minds and bodies. Then they can start to visualize their ideal future.

Introverts can imagine themselves in specific situations or scenarios that are aligned with their goals. For example, if an introvert wants to excel in their career, they can visualize themselves confidently giving presentations, leading teams, or networking with ease. They can vividly imagine the details of these scenarios, such as the sights, sounds, and feelings associated with them. By engaging their senses, introverts can make their visualizations more powerful and immersive.

As introverts continue to practice visualization, they can gradually expand their vision to include different aspects of their life, such as relationships, personal growth, and well-being. They can imagine themselves surrounded by supportive and uplifting people, experiencing joy and fulfillment in their personal relationships. They can envision themselves pursuing their passions, overcoming challenges, and achieving meaningful milestones in their personal and professional development.

Visualization can also be used to overcome limiting beliefs and self-doubt. If an introvert is holding on to negative thoughts or beliefs about themselves, they can visualize themselves letting go of these limiting beliefs and replacing them with positive affirmations. By repeatedly visualizing positive outcomes and challenging their negative beliefs, introverts can rewire their brains and cultivate a more optimistic and empowered mindset.

It's important for introverts to regularly engage in visualization exercises to reinforce their vision and goals. They can set aside dedicated time each day or week to practice visualization techniques. Whether it's spending a few minutes before bed or incorporating visualization into a morning routine, consistency is key in harnessing the power of visualization.

By visualizing their success and aligning their actions with their vision, introverts can create a meaningful and fulfilling life that is true to their authentic selves. Visualization can help introverts stay focused, motivated, and resilient in the face of challenges. With a clear and positive vision, introverts can confidently navigate the challenging extroverted environment and create their own version of success. So take the time to close your eyes, quiet your mind, and visualize the future you desire. Your introverted success is within reach.

THE VISION-DRIVEN GOAL SETTING MODEL FOR INTROVERTS (VDGSM)

The Vision-Driven Goal Setting Model for Introverts (VDGSM) is a comprehensive framework designed to help introverts create a positive vision for their future and set actionable goals that align with their unique strengths and values. This model consists of three key components: creating a positive vision, alignment with introverted strengths, and setting SMART goals. Let's explore each component in detail:

CREATING A POSITIVE VISION

The first step in the VDGSM is to create a positive vision for your future. This involves leveraging the power of visualization to imagine your ideal life with vivid detail. As an introvert, you can tap into your innate strengths of introspection and deep thinking to explore what success and fulfillment mean to you personally. Visualize not only the external achievements you desire, but also the feelings and emotions that come with them.

Creating a positive vision is an individual journey that involves looking within yourself and contemplating. Dedicate some moments to ponder what genuinely holds significance for you in your personal and work lives. Reflect on your beliefs, interests, and areas of expertise. Imagine a future where you are immersed in a lifestyle that resonates with these parts of who you are.

ALIGNMENT WITH INTROVERTED STRENGTHS

Once you've created a positive vision, the next step is to figure out how your introverted qualities can help you reach your objectives. Introverts possess traits such as deep thinking, sustained concentration, and laser focus that can drive their achievements. By connecting your aspirations with these strengths, you can harness them to tackle challenges and move closer to realizing your dreams.

For example, if your vision includes becoming a published author, you can tap into your introverted nature to craft engaging ideas for your writing. Utilize your skills for contemplation and focus to fuel your writing process. By aligning your goals with your introverted qualities, you can maximize your prospects for achievement and derive satisfaction along the way.

SETTING SMART GOALS

Dr. Gladys West was a mathematician and introverted trailblazer whose work on an incredibly precise model for the shape of the Earth was critical to the development of GPS technology. By setting clear, measurable goals aligned with her vision, she made groundbreaking contributions despite working behind the scenes.

When you establish SMART goals, it's crucial to break them down into smaller, manageable tasks. This approach not only reduces the feeling of being overwhelmed but also enhances the likelihood of accomplishing your objectives. By creating realistic deadlines and milestones, you can keep yourself on course. Consistently contemplate your goals to guarantee they stay in line with your aspirations and make modifications as needed.

By following the VDGSM, introverts can develop a clear roadmap for success that is grounded in their unique strengths and values. This model emphasizes the importance of reflection, adaptation, and perseverance, enabling introverts to pursue their goals with composure and candidness. Remember, success is a personal and individual concept that should be defined by you, not solely by societal standards. Embrace your introverted nature and embark on a journey toward your own unique version of success.

EMBRACING YOUR UNIQUE PATH TO SUCCESS

As you near the close of this chapter, keep in mind that there is **no cookie-cutter approach to success**. It's a personal journey that you mold to fit your needs. You can create a path that is authentic to you by rethinking success and how it relates to your values and goals.

You may experience times of doubt and anxiety along this journey. Remember to **practice self-compassion** at these moments. Do yourself the favor of being kind and patient, just as you would a friend. Accept that obstacles will arise and have faith in your capacity to conquer them. Treat yourself kindly, and give yourself props for being brave enough to follow your path.

PAINTING A PICTURE OF YOUR DREAMS

Using **visualization can be a powerful tool** in clarifying your dreams and goals. When you imagine yourself attaining your objectives, it can help you create a plan of action. Your positive vision will direct you toward your goals with focus and persistence.

TURNING DREAMS INTO REALITY WITH COMMITMENT

As we discussed earlier, SMART goals is the final step in the VDGSM. However, setting **SMART goals** is not just about having a to-do list; it's about creating a roadmap to bring your vision to life and setting yourself up for success. Each small step you take toward your goals brings you closer to the fulfilling future you've envisioned.

Facing challenges and setbacks is a part of pursuing goals, but they don't have to stop you in your tracks. Instead of letting failures discourage you, **reframe them as opportunities** for development and improvement. Ask yourself, 'What can I learn from this experience?' and 'How can I approach this differently next time?' By looking at failures from this perspective, you can uncover lessons that will help you advance along your path.

As you start on this voyage of self-exploration and goal-setting, remember that the road to success is yours to shape. Having a vision, setting SMART goals, and staying dedicated to your dreams will lead you toward the success that truly speaks to your heart. Allow your brilliance to illuminate your journey towards a fulfilling and authentic life. *Believe in yourself and your ability to create a success story that is uniquely yours.*

Surrounding yourself with a supportive network can be invaluable for maintaining a positive mindset. Whether it's joining a local meetup group, finding an online community, or confiding in trusted friends or family members, having **a support system** can provide the encouragement and accountability you need to overcome challenges and stay motivated.

NEXT UP

You've redefined what success means to you, developed a vision that ignites your passions, and set SMART goals to propel you ahead. However, the path to success is not always clear. There will be challenges, failures, and moments when you question yourself. This is when the power of positive thinking takes center stage. In Chapter 8: The Positivity Pathway, we'll discuss how to cultivate an optimistic mindset that fuels your resilience and allows you to overcome any obstacles that come your way. We will look at ways for developing self-compassion and harnessing the power of gratitude. By maintaining a positive attitude, you will be better able to persevere in the face of adversity and appreciate your victories, big and small, as you go forward. Remember that having a positive mindset gives you a hidden advantage on the path to achieving your introverted version of success.

CHAPTER 8

THE POSITIVITY PATHWAY

Jasper lingered by the window, his gaze settling on a garden where morning dew clung to the leaves like a tender promise. His room carried a stillness broken only by the occasional song of a robin searching for its morning meal. Today, he was determined to pluck the splinters of discontent from his heart, replacing them with gratitude.

He reflected on the words of his grandmother, a woman whose eyes seemed to weave sunlight even as age crept upon her like twilight shadows. "Gratitude," she'd say, her voice soft as the first snow, "is the flower that blooms from the seeds of trouble."

The aroma of the earth after rain filled the room, a subtle yet potent reminder of nature's enduring cycle of regeneration. Jasper's chest rose with a deep breath, and as he exhaled, he imagined releasing the weights of doubt that had anchored him for so long. He had practiced this form of mindfulness before, a dance of breath and release, where worrisome thoughts swirled away like leaves in a stream.

A distant laughter echoed from the street below, slicing through his introspection. It was boisterous and filled with a community spirit Jasper often admired but participated in from afar. He was the quiet observer, the introvert who found solace in reflection. Challenges often loomed larger for him, their shadows stretching and mingling with his own doubts.

Today, though, he sought the ray of sunshine in these shadows. He recognized that within his introspective nature there was a wellspring of strength, an untapped reservoir of creativity and depth. He squared his shoulders, feeling a surge of determination. Every challenge was an opportunity for growth, a chance to embark on a journey of self-discovery and turn vulnerability into victory.

With a newfound sense of purpose, he began to tidy his space, his movements purposeful and filled with intention. Each object had a story, a memory attached, and as he dusted and sorted, he acknowledged the journey that brought him to this moment. He was cultivating not just a cleaner living space but also a sanctuary for his thoughts and dreams.

The pages of his journal fluttered as a breeze slipped through the cracked window, their rustling like whispers spurring him onward. He settled at his desk, hands hovering over the creamy sheets. Today, he would write about the positive, he decided. He would fill these pages with the quiet triumphs and joys that often went unnoticed. With each word, his spirit lifted, lightened by the acknowledgment of life's simple beauty.

In the quiet hum of a day unfolding, swathed in the golden light of morning, Jasper found his heart. It beat with a rhythm that acknowledged life's ebullient and despairing melodies. What more, he wondered, could gratitude reveal to him if he simply gave it the stage?

DISCOVER THE SUNSHINE AFTER THE STORM

Navigating life as an introvert in a world that often feels designed for the extrovert can feel akin to a fish learning to climb a tree—

it's entirely possible, but boy, does it require a shift in perspective! The knack of turning challenges into opportunities and focusing on gratitude can indeed make that tree climb seem like a thrilling adventure rather than an insurmountable obstacle. Imagine, just for a moment, how transforming your mindset could not only illuminate your path but make the journey exhilarating.

Cultivating gratitude isn't just about saying thank you. It's a practice akin to watering a garden; the more you nurture it, the more bountiful your harvest. It's about waking up and recognizing the good in your day, no matter how small. Studies have shown that individuals who practice gratitude regularly experience more positive emotions, feel more alive, sleep better, express more compassion and kindness, and even have stronger immune systems. For introverts, this practice can be a game-changer. It shifts the focus from what's depleting to what's replenishing. It makes the challenges of daily navigation less daunting in a social landscape that may force introverts to feel that they need to pretend to fit in.

Finding the silver lining is an art and a practice that turns life's lemons into a zest for life. It's easy to focus on the roadblocks, but what if we viewed them as stepping stones instead? This shift in perspective helps introverts see hurdles as opportunities for growth, personal development, and ultimately, a more fulfilling life. By reframing challenges, we open the door to new possibilities and adventures that previously seemed out of reach. This approach not only fosters resilience but also builds a kind of inner strength that is not easily shaken by the world's demands.

THE QUIET STRENGTH OF THE PRESENT MOMENT

Practicing mindfulness is about embracing the present with all its nuances and colors. It's about tuning into the now, fully experiencing the moment without judgment. For introverts, this can mean acknowledging their feelings and thoughts but

93

choosing to focus on the positive aspects of their current situation. Mindfulness techniques—be it through meditation, deep breathing, or even mindful walking—encourage a state of balance and peace that can significantly reduce stress and anxiety. This daily practice helps introverts to cultivate inner peace, enhancing their ability to navigate the external world with a sense of calm and centeredness.

Imagine, for instance, the power of starting your day not with a sense of dread for the challenges ahead but with a moment of mindfulness, acknowledging the beauty of the sunrise or the calm of the morning. This simple act sets the tone for a day viewed through a lens of positivity and possibility.

THE POSITIVITY POTION FOR EVERYDAY LIFE

In the journey of harnessing optimism, introverts have a unique advantage—their introspective nature. This characteristic, often misunderstood as a limitation, is actually a superpower when aligned with positive thinking and gratitude. It allows for a deeper connection with oneself, fostering a nurturing environment for growth and optimism.

Here are some practical strategies for integrating the practices of gratitude, finding the positive spin, and putting mindfulness into your daily routine:

1. **Keep a gratitude journal**: Each day, jot down three things you're thankful for. They can be as simple as a delicious cup of coffee or as significant as the love of a friend.
2. **Challenge negative thoughts**: When faced with a challenge, stop and ask yourself, "What can I learn from this? How can this make me stronger or more empathetic?"
3. **Take mindfulness breaks**: Throughout your day, take short breaks to simply breathe and be present. Even three deep breaths can reset your mind and reduce stress.

4. **Savor the small moments**: Whether it's the warmth of sunlight on your skin or the taste of your favorite food, taking time to appreciate the small joys in life can significantly boost your mood.
5. **Connect with nature**: Spending time in natural surroundings can help clear your mind and foster a sense of peace and gratitude.
6. **Practice kindness**: Acts of kindness, whether toward yourself or others, can have a profound impact on your well-being and outlook on life.

By incorporating these practices into your life, you cultivate a Positivity Pathway that not only enriches your inner world but also transforms how you navigate the external one. The journey of positive thinking and gratitude for introverts is not about changing who you are. Rather, it's about enhancing your life experience by focusing on the beauty and opportunities that abound, turning what might seem like an extrovert world into a playground for growth, resilience, and fulfillment.

As introverts, we often find ourselves prone to overthinking and dwelling on negative experiences. It can be easy to get caught up in a cycle of self-doubt and criticism, which can leave us feeling drained and overwhelmed. But what if I told you that there was a simple practice that could help shift our focus toward the positive aspects of our lives?

This practice is gratitude. By cultivating gratitude, introverts can foster optimism and inner strength. It involves recognizing and appreciating the good things in our lives, no matter how small they may seem. When we intentionally focus on what we are grateful for, we nourish a positive mindset and build resilience.

Gratitude can be practiced in many ways. It can be as simple as starting a gratitude journal, where you write down three things you are grateful for each day. It can also involve expressing gratitude to others, whether through a heartfelt thank you or a handwritten note. By actively engaging in these practices, we train our minds to notice and appreciate the positive aspects of our lives.

Research has shown that gratitude has numerous benefits for our well-being. It can increase our overall happiness and life satisfaction, improve our physical health, enhance our relationships, and even boost our resilience in the face of challenges. When we focus on what we are grateful for, we shift our attention away from our problems and toward solutions. We are better able to reframe challenges as opportunities for growth, and this ultimately leads to a more fulfilling and confident life journey.

It's important to note that practicing gratitude doesn't mean ignoring or denying the negative aspects of our lives. It simply means choosing to focus on the positive, no matter how small it may seem. By cultivating gratitude, introverts can develop a more optimistic outlook on life and build the resilience necessary to navigate the challenges we face.

Let's embark on the path of gratitude together. In the next section, we will explore strategies to help introverts find the bright side in challenges and discover opportunities for growth. By combining the power of gratitude with a mindset of resilience, introverts can truly prosper in a culture that often undervalues the contributions of quiet thinkers and observers.

STRATEGIES FOR REFRAMING CHALLENGES AND FINDING OPPORTUNITIES

In life, we all encounter challenges. Dealing with those problems, especially as an introvert, can be daunting at times. However, by adjusting our perspective and reframing these challenges, we might uncover chances for growth and self-improvement. Here are some techniques to help you recognize the positive aspects of difficult situations.

1. **Embrace the Power of Perspective:**
   Our perception of challenges often shapes our reactions to them. When we change our viewpoint, we can discover an optimistic outlook in even the toughest times. For instance, when encountering a setback in your career, instead of seeing it as a failure, you could regard it as a chance to reassess your goals and uncover new opportunities. By altering your perspective, you can transform obstacles into building blocks toward a more fulfilling career path.

2. **Practice Gratitude:**
   Gratitude is a powerful tool that can direct our focus toward the positive aspects of our lives, even in difficult situations. Set aside a few minutes daily to ponder on what you're grateful for, be it the love from family and friends, a beautiful sunset, or even a minor achievement. Nurturing gratitude helps to foster optimism and resilience, enabling us to see the silver linings amidst challenges.

3. **Embrace Failure as a Learning Opportunity:**
   Accepting setbacks as learning experiences is essential because failure is inevitable. Think of these challenges as stepping stones to success rather than reflections of your ability. Take the time to figure out what went wrong and apply what you've learned to improve your skills and decision-making going forward. Remember that you are getting closer to triumph with every setback.

4. **Seek Support from Others:**
   When you encounter obstacles, always remember that you have a support system. Don't hesitate to lean on friends, family members, or mentors for advice and encouragement. Sometimes discussing your challenges with someone who

empathizes can offer insights or uncover solutions you might not have thought of independently.

5. **Practice Self-Reflection**:

   Engaging in self-reflection can be really beneficial for development as it allows you to discover areas for improvements amidst difficulties. Make sure to allocate some time to reflect on your experiences, feelings, and responses. Consider what lessons you can draw from each challenge and how you leverage that insight to evolve and enhance yourself. Knowing your strengths and weaknesses enables you to tackle obstacles with efficiency.

6. **Embrace Change:**

   Change can be daunting, but it also presents new opportunities for growth and personal development. Instead of pushing against change, welcome it as an opportunity to rediscover yourself and venture into uncharted territories. Keep in mind that every change carries the potential for progress and positive transformation.

7. **Celebrate Small Victories:**

   When faced with difficulties, it's common to dwell on the negative and concentrate only on the hurdles in front of you. Yet by cherishing wins throughout the journey, you can keep a positive outlook and gain momentum. Be it finishing a challenging task or conquering a fear, make sure to recognize and rejoice in your successes, regardless of how minor they may appear.

Keanu Reeves exemplifies embracing change and transforming challenges into opportunities for growth. Despite encountering personal hardships and career setbacks, Reeves has shown resilience and a willingness to explore new avenues. He has taken on diverse roles, both in mainstream and independent films, constantly evolving as an actor and an individual.

By reframing challenges and finding opportunities for growth, you can foster resilience and embrace the positivity that life has to offer. Remember, every challenge is an opportunity for personal development and a chance to become a stronger, more confident version of yourself. Recognize the opportunities for growth within challenges and approach life's obstacles with a positive and resilient mindset.

OVERCOMING ROADBLOCKS: GUIDE TO PERSEVERING ON THE POSITIVITY PATHWAY

While the practices of gratitude, reframing challenges, and mindfulness can be immensely beneficial for introverts, it's important to acknowledge that the journey toward a more positive mindset may not always be smooth sailing. Introverts may face unique roadblocks or challenges along the way, such as:

1. **Overthinking and rumination**: As deep thinkers, introverts may find themselves caught in cycles of overthinking or rumination, which can make it difficult to shift their focus toward gratitude or a more positive perspective.

   To overcome this, try setting a time limit for introspection and then consciously shifting your attention to the present moment through mindfulness techniques like deep breathing or grounding exercises.

2. **Social comparison and self-doubt**: In a world that frequently praises extroverted personalities, introverted individuals might find it challenging to overcome self-doubt or feelings of inadequacy, making it harder for them to recognize their talents and nurture a sense of gratitude.

   Counter these negative thoughts by practicing self-compassion and affirmations. Remind yourself of your unique qualities and achievements and celebrate the small wins along the way.

3. **Difficulty in letting go**: For some introverts, letting go of negative experiences, emotions, or thought patterns can be a challenge, making it harder to reframe challenges or embrace a more positive mindset.

   Try incorporating mindfulness practices like body scans or visualization exercises to help you release tension and negative energy. Additionally, journaling can be a powerful tool for processing and letting go of difficult experiences.

4. **Resistance to change**: Introverts may find comfort in routine and familiarity, which can sometimes lead to resistance to change or new practices like gratitude, reframing, or mindfulness.

   Start small, and be patient with yourself. Gradually incorporate these practices into your daily routine, and celebrate each step as a victory. Remember that change takes time, and it's okay to go at your own pace.

5. **Feeling overwhelmed**: With so many techniques and strategies to explore, some introverts may feel overwhelmed or unsure of where to begin their journey to a more positive mindset.

   Start by identifying your most meaningful practice and work on mastering that one technique at a time. Remember that progress, not perfection, is what matters most, and seek advice from those who are experienced with these disciplines.

By acknowledging and addressing these potential roadblocks, introverts can overcome the challenges that may arise on their journey toward cultivating gratitude, reframing challenges, and practicing mindfulness. Remember, perseverance and self-compassion are key, and with time and consistency, these practices can become invaluable tools for fostering resilience, optimism, and a more fulfilling life.

PRACTICING MINDFULNESS: FINDING INNER PEACE AND BALANCE

In the hustle and bustle of our social world, introverts may often feel stressed and isolated. For this reason, introverts may find that practicing mindfulness helps them find inner peace and harmony. Mindfulness involves staying in the moment and being conscious of one's thoughts, emotions, and physical sensations without judgment. Adding meditation and other forms of mindfulness practice into their daily routines can help introverts draw on their inner resources and see the positive side of life.

Starting your mindfulness practice involves establishing a routine. This could mean dedicating a few moments each morning to sit peacefully and concentrate on your breathing. By starting your day with a purposeful pause, you establish an atmosphere for the hours ahead. Additionally, integrating mindfulness into your everyday activities, like walking, eating, or even managing household chores can deepen your connection to the moment and release any unnecessary distractions.

EXPLORING ADDITIONAL MINDFULNESS TECHNIQUES

While mindful breathing and mindful walking are excellent starting points for cultivating present-moment awareness, there are numerous other mindfulness techniques that can be valuable additions to an introvert's toolkit. Here are a few to explore:

1. **Body Scans**: A body scan is a mindfulness practice that involves systematically directing your attention to different parts of your body, noticing any sensations, tension, or areas of relaxation. This technique can help you cultivate a

deeper connection with your physical self and release stored tension or stress.

Start by getting yourself into a comfortable seated or lying position and take some deep breaths. Next, gradually focus your awareness on parts of your body, beginning at your toes and moving up to the top of your head. Be mindful of any feelings without judgment, and deliberately release any tension in each area as you progress through the scan.

2. **Loving-Kindness Meditation**: Warmth, empathy, and kindness toward oneself and others can be developed by regular practice of this form of meditation. Introverts, who may struggle to overcome social anxiety, may find it very beneficial.

   Begin by finding a comfortable seated position and taking a few deep breaths. Then bring to mind someone you genuinely care about and silently repeat phrases of well-wishing, such as "May you be happy, may you be healthy, may you be safe, may you live with ease." After a few minutes, direct these phrases toward yourself and, eventually, toward all beings everywhere.

3. **Mindful Eating**: Engaging in mindful eating involves focusing entirely on the act of enjoying food, relishing each mouthful, and recognizing the tastes, textures, and nourishment it offers. This habit can help you develop a healthier relationship with food and elevate your overall mindfulness practice routine.

   Take a few moments to appreciate the colors, smells and textures of your meal or snack before you dive in. Take your time and focus on chewing every bite. Pay attention to the tastes and sensations that arise in the here and now.

Redirect your attention back to the pleasure of eating if you find that your mind wanders.

These additional mindfulness techniques can deepen your practice and provide you with a diverse toolkit to cultivate present-moment awareness, self-compassion, and a more positive mindset. Remember, mindfulness is a journey, and exploring different practices can help you find the ones that resonate most with your personal preferences and needs as an introvert.

Oprah Winfrey, one of the most influential personalities in the media industry, has been known for promoting the importance of mindfulness. Through her interviews and writings, she has expressed the benefits of incorporating a mindfulness practice like meditation and journaling into her routine to maintain balance and concentration in the midst of her busy and diverse professional responsibilities.

Self-care plays an important role in mindfulness for introverts. It's not about being selfish; it's about looking after yourself to stay healthy. Introverts typically need moments of solitude to rejuvenate and reflect. By dedicating time to engage in self-care activities like reading, soaking in a bath, or strolling amidst nature, you can nurture your mind, body, and spirit. Remember, for introverts, self-care isn't an indulgence; it's vital for flourishing.

Mindfulness can also help introverts manage their energy levels. We all have limited energy reserves, and introverts can easily become drained by social interactions. By being mindful of how certain activities or people affect your energy, you can make choices that align with your needs. This might mean politely declining invitations to social events when you need to recharge or setting boundaries with others to protect your energy.

Additionally, introverts can benefit from practicing mindfulness by shifting their attention from negative self-talk to positive self-affirmation. A great deal of control over our emotions and actions is exerted by our thoughts. Mindfulness practice allows us to step back and objectively assess our thoughts, giving us the power to choose whether to internalize negative or positive ones. Take the example of choosing to recognize the lesson learned and the progress accomplished rather than getting stuck on a perceived mistake. Optimism and resilience in the face of adversity may result from this shift in viewpoint.

And lastly, mindfulness can assist introverts in cultivating gratitude. Gratitude involves recognizing and valuing the positive aspects of our lives. By concentrating on things we are thankful for, we teach our minds to notice the positives, even during tough times. This approach can help introverts to reframe challenges as opportunities for growth and nurture a positive outlook on life.

In conclusion, mindfulness is an invaluable practice for introverts to find inner peace and balance in an environment that rewards those who think out loud. By creating a daily ritual, practicing self-care, managing energy levels, reframing negative thoughts, and cultivating gratitude, introverts can tap into their inner strength, foster resilience, and navigate life's challenges with optimism. Remember, practicing mindfulness is an ongoing journey, so be patient with yourself and accept the process. With a mindful approach, introverts can create a more fulfilling and confident life.

EMBRACING THE POSITIVITY PATHWAY

As we reflect on the journey through the Positivity Pathway, it becomes evident that each step is a building block toward a more optimistic and resilient mindset. **Cultivating gratitude** serves as the cornerstone, allowing us to appreciate the beauty in our lives, even during challenging times. Finding a ray of optimism empowers us to see obstacles as opportunities for growth, transforming setbacks into stepping stones to success. **Practicing mindfulness** grounds us in the present moment, fostering inner peace and balance amidst the chaos of everyday life.

THE POWER OF POSITIVE THINKING

By integrating these techniques into our lives, we unlock a perspective that transforms obstacles into opportunities, fear into courage, and uncertainty into resolve. Through **gratitude**, we sow the seeds of contentment and joy in our hearts, nurturing a sense of fulfillment that transcends circumstances. **Reframing challenges** allows us to rise above difficulties, seeing them not as roadblocks but as detours leading to unexpected horizons of growth and self-discovery. **Mindfulness** becomes our guiding compass, steering us to a place of quiet strength and unwavering resilience in the face of life's storms.

As you move forward in life, always keep in mind that the Positivity Pathway is more than a guide; it's a mindset—a way of thinking that can transform how you see the world and your role in it. By embracing gratitude, looking for the bright light at the end of the tunnel, and practicing mindfulness, you can create a path illuminated by hope, courage, and unwavering optimism.

YOUR PATH TO OPTIMISM

Let **gratitude** be your daily companion, enriching your life with blessings big and small. Train your mind to see the bright side, to find the **silver lining** in every cloud that passes overhead. Practice **mindfulness** as you navigate the complexities of modern life, grounding yourself in the present moment and nurturing a sense of calm amidst the chaos.

Incorporate these practices into your daily routine, and watch as your world transforms before your eyes. *Remember, the power of positive thinking lies not in denying reality but in choosing how we respond to it. With each step you take along the Positivity Pathway, you equip yourself with the tools needed to thrive, grow, and flourish in a world that can be exhausting and often feels overwhelming to introverts.*

Let optimism light your path, brightening even the darkest corners with hope for a better future. Walk forward with certainty, trusting in your strength, perseverance, and inner wisdom to conquer any challenges that you encounter. *May your journey be filled with moments of gratitude, opportunities for growth, and a deep sense of peace that comes from knowing you are right where you belong.*

NEXT UP

The practices explored in the Positivity Pathway—gratitude, reframing challenges, and mindfulness—have all contributed to building your inner strength and resilience. This newfound strength is the foundation for effective networking skills. Think about it—gratitude allows you to approach others with a genuine appreciation for their experiences. Reframing challenges allows you to see networking events not as hurdles but as opportunities to connect and learn. And mindfulness equips you to be present in conversations, fostering authentic interactions.

In the next chapter, we'll see how these very qualities translate into effective networking skills. We'll delve into strategies for initiating conversations, building rapport with diverse personalities, and leveraging the power of networking for success. Remember, the skills you've cultivated on the Positivity Pathway are the secret weapons that will help you thrive in the world of networking.

CHAPTER 9

EXPLORING THE
NETWORKING EXPERIENCE

The sun slanted through the blinds, casting striped shadows across the room where Thomas sat, a solitary figure at a sparsely decorated desk. On his computer screen flickered the remnants of an online networking seminar designed for those who thrived in the quiet. The words, though meant to empower, seemed distant and faint, like birdsong heard through closed windows. He closed his eyes briefly, inhaling the faint scent of lemon oil from the polished wood before him. The stillness of the room was a comfort—unlike the clamoring, shoulder-to-shoulder spaces where networking tended to thrive.

His mind wandered back to his university days, when classmates chattered like sparrows while he watched, a silent owl amidst the foliage. He remembered the ease with which they darted from branch to branch, from one social circle to another, while he longed for the intimacy of one-on-one discussions that never came to be. The task ahead loomed like a mountain, cast in the sharp relief of the evening light.

A soft buzz from his phone interrupted the quiet, a message from a colleague suggesting a small gathering among people with shared interests in sustainable technologies. Thomas considered this, the idea settling like a gentle weight in his chest. To foster genuine connections, to find kinship in shared values—it felt right, much like the worn pages of a favored book held tightly in one's grasp.

He stood up, pacing the room, hands clasped behind him. The familiarity of his surroundings—walls adorned with the minimalist art he cherished, the weight of the books in his shelves—reassured him. He contemplated the idea that in the smaller gatherings, in discussions deeply rooted in shared passions, he might just find his tribe.

Perhaps, Thomas pondered, the key lay not in changing his nature, but in leveraging it. Online platforms where discussions flowed without the pressure of immediate response, where thoughtfulness was currency, beckoned to him. In the digital realm, words were his allies, and the quiet contemplation that introversion afforded could be woven into the very fabric of his connections.

Could it be that the bonds forged in the crucible of genuine interest were stronger than the brittle connections born of chance encounters? Thomas halted his pacing and allowed a small smile. It was a thought that warmed him from within—like the sun's rays finally breaking through a persistent cloud cover.

A glance at his watch told Thomas it was time for his weekly walk through the park, a ritual of reflection amid nature's whispers. He grabbed his jacket, anticipating the rustle of leaves above and the gentle crunch underfoot. As his hand turned the doorknob, he realized that some strategies for reaching out were not a shouting into the void but rather a conversation within a quiet room filled with like-minded souls.

In the embrace of the day's fading light, Thomas began to understand that networking need not be a masked ball where you danced until dizzy. It could be like the park he strolled through—a place where each tree stood tall and singular, yet part of a greater whole. With every step, he asked himself: if the value of connections lies not in their number but in their depth, what worlds could open when one acknowledged this truth?

UNLOCKING THE POWER OF INTROVERTED NETWORKING

When it comes to networking, the common imagery that springs to mind might be bustling conferences or loud, crowded social events—environments where extroversion seems not just beneficial but necessary. However, this perspective overlooks the profound strengths introverts bring to the table, especially in the realm of making authentic connections. This insight is particularly crucial in understanding that networking is not just about collecting contacts but about forging meaningful relationships based on shared values and interests. Such relationships prove to be the cornerstone of both personal growth and professional success.

Introversion, often misunderstood as shyness or antisocial behavior, is actually a wellspring of networking prowess. Introverts are naturally inclined toward deep, meaningful conversations rather than surface-level small talk. This preference positions them perfectly to create connections that are not just numerous but rich in quality and potential. By embracing this innate inclination, introverts can navigate the networking world in a way that aligns with their strengths rather than against them.

CRAFTING GENUINE CONNECTIONS

The journey starts by **exploring networking strategies tailored to introverted preferences.** This involves seeking out one-on-one conversations or online networking opportunities. The digital realm, in particular, offers a plethora of platforms for introverts to connect with like-minded individuals without the overwhelming energy of in-person events. It's not about the quantity of connections made but the quality. Focusing on fewer, more meaningful interactions leads to stronger, more beneficial professional relationships.

Another pivotal step is **identifying shared interests and values**. Building relationships on common ground not only ensures authenticity but also longevity. Initiating conversations by seeking out these commonalities fosters a genuine connection from the get-go. Conversation starters and questions that dig deeper into personal and professional values can enrich this connection further, paving the way for relationships that extend beyond mere acquaintance.

THE DIGITAL HANDSHAKE

In today's world, **utilizing online platforms** for networking is not just convenient for introverts; it's strategic. The ability to connect from one's own comfort zone allows for more thoughtful interactions. Finding communities and platforms that align with specific interests or professional goals can open doors to relationships that might never have been accessible in a traditional networking setting.

When venturing into **one-on-one settings**, preparation is key. Thinking ahead about topics of conversation or goals for the meeting can alleviate the anxiety that often accompanies face-to-face interactions. Active listening and engaging through open-ended questions can transform these meetings from nerve-wracking to enriching experiences.

SETTING A PATH FOR GROWTH

With these strategies in hand, **setting realistic goals** becomes the foundation for successful networking endeavors. Whether it's attending a specific number of events, making a certain amount of new connections, or simply having deeper conversations with existing contacts, clear objectives guide fruitful networking efforts.

Following up and maintaining professional connections is crucial. Simple gestures like personalized emails or scheduling regular check-ins can strengthen professional relationships significantly. This ongoing effort turns initial meetings into lasting affiliations.

Lastly, **seeking support and feedback** from mentors or peers can enhance networking skills. Coupled with **self-reflection and growth**, this feedback loop encourages continuous improvement and adaptation of networking approaches. Recognizing areas for growth and celebrating successes fuels a cycle of positive development in networking abilities and confidence.

NAVIGATING NETWORKING: A GUIDE FOR THE INTROVERTED PROFESSIONAL

1. **Explore Introverted Networking Strategies**: Lean into platforms and settings that complement the introverted way of engagement.
2. **Identify Shared Interests and Values**: Use common ground as the cornerstone for building meaningful connections.
3. **Utilize Online Platforms**: Leverage the digital space to connect in a less energy-draining manner.
4. **Prepare for One-on-One Settings**: Equip yourself with conversation starters and active listening skills for deeper interactions.
5. **Set Realistic Goals**: Define what success looks like for you in networking to keep track of progress.
6. **Follow Up and Maintain Connections**: Keep the conversation going with thoughtful follow-ups and regular check-ins.
7. **Seek Support and Feedback**: Use insights from mentors and peers to refine your networking strategy.

8. **Practice Self-Reflection and Growth**: Continuously evaluate your networking experiences to recognize achievements and areas for improvement.

By embracing these principles, the journey through the networking landscape can transform from a daunting endeavor into a rewarding pathway to growth and success.

PREPARING FOR LARGER NETWORKING EVENTS

Here are some tips and exercises to help introverts prepare mentally and emotionally for larger networking events:

Mental Preparation:

1. **Reframe Your Mindset**: Instead of viewing networking as a daunting task, reframe it as an opportunity to meet interesting individuals and learn from their experiences. Remind yourself that you have valuable insights and perspectives to share as well.
2. **Set Realistic Goals**: Don't overwhelm yourself by aiming to meet and connect with everyone. Set manageable goals, such as having meaningful conversations with two or three people or simply practicing your networking skills.
3. **Visualize Success**: Engage in positive visualization techniques. Imagine yourself feeling confident, engaging in stimulating conversations, and making meaningful connections. This mental rehearsal can boost your self-assurance.

Emotional Preparation:

1. **Practice Self-Care**: Before the event, engage in activities that help you feel grounded and centered. This could include meditation, deep breathing exercises, or engaging in a favorite hobby.

2. **Identify Your Strengths**: Make a list of your unique qualities, skills, and accomplishments. Remind yourself of the value you bring to conversations and connections.

3. **Role-Play**: Get some practice introducing yourself, striking up conversations, and asking open-ended questions from someone you trust. Taking part in this exercise can make you feel more at ease and assured when the big day arrives.

4. **Plan Breaks**: Networking events can be emotionally draining for introverts. Plan to take short breaks during the event to recharge. Find a quiet corner or step outside for a few minutes of solitude before re-engaging.

5. **Bring a Supportive Friend**: If possible, attend the event with a friend or colleague who understands and supports your introverted nature. They can provide a sense of familiarity and help you navigate social situations.

6. **Celebrate Small Wins**: After the event, acknowledge and celebrate even the smallest successes, such as making eye contact, introducing yourself, or engaging in a brief conversation. This positive reinforcement can help build confidence for future networking opportunities.

Remember, networking is a skill that can be developed with practice and preparation. By taking steps to manage your mental and emotional state, you can approach these events with greater confidence and resilience.

NAVIGATING NETWORKING HURDLES: STRATEGIES FOR INTROVERTS

While the strategies outlined in this chapter can empower introverts to navigate the networking landscape with confidence, it's important to acknowledge the potential challenges and roadblocks that may arise. Two common hurdles that introverts often face are social anxiety and difficulty initiating conversations.

Social Anxiety: For many introverts, the thought of attending networking events or engaging in social interactions can trigger feelings of anxiety or discomfort. This is a natural response, as introverts tend to derive their energy from solitude and may find large social gatherings draining. To overcome this challenge, consider the following strategies:

1. **Practice self-care**: Before attending a networking event, engage in activities that help you feel grounded and centered, such as meditation, deep breathing exercises, or simply taking a quiet walk.
2. **Set realistic goals**: Instead of overwhelming yourself with the expectation of meeting countless new people, set a modest goal, such as having one or two meaningful conversations.
3. **Bring a friend or colleague**: Having someone you know around can bring a feeling of ease and encouragement, making it simpler to interact with others.

Difficulty Initiating Conversations: Introverts may struggle with initiating conversations, especially in situations where they don't know anyone. However, with a bit of preparation and practice, this challenge can be overcome:

1. **Prepare conversation starters**: Research the event or the industry you'll be networking in, and prepare a few open-ended questions or topics that can help kick-start a conversation.
2. **Practice active listening**: When someone is speaking, focus on truly listening and asking follow-up questions based on what they've shared. This can help keep the conversation flowing naturally.
3. **Leverage shared interests**: If you know attendees' backgrounds or interests, use that information to find common ground and initiate a conversation around those shared interests.

Always bear in mind that networking is an acquired talent. Take your time, celebrate even the smallest successes, and don't be shy about seeking advice from people you respect or those who have been successful in networking. Even introverts can benefit from networking if they are willing to put in the work and aren't afraid to try new things.

By acknowledging common challenges and providing practical strategies for overcoming them, this section will help introverted readers feel more prepared and equipped to navigate the networking landscape with confidence and resilience.

Networking events can be intimidating for introverts, as they may find it challenging to navigate through large crowds and engage in conversations. However, it's crucial to bear in mind that networking isn't exclusively tailored for extroverted individuals. In reality, introverts have the potential to forge connections by capitalizing on their unique qualities. By recognizing your personality traits and leveraging them during networking events, you can formulate approaches that align with your introverted strengths and foster genuine connections.

Just as in personal relationships discussed in Chapter 4, one strategy is to focus on quality over quantity. Instead of trying to meet as many people as possible, introverts can thrive by nurturing deep connections with a select few individuals. Take the time to listen and engage in meaningful conversations, rather than engaging in surface-level interactions. By forging these authentic connections, you are more likely to find networking success that aligns with your values and interests.

For introverts, a great approach is to attend networking events that match their passions and interests. When you have an interest in a subject or field, it's simpler to participate in discussions and connect with like-minded individuals. Seek out events and groups that focus on topics that truly excite you, as this will set the stage for meaningful conversations and valuable connections.

Introverts can also use their reflective nature to their benefit during networking. Spend some time thinking about your objectives and what you hope to gain from networking events. Consider what holds significance for you and how you can genuinely engage with others who share similar goals. By approaching networking with intention and purpose, introverts can forge connections that are advantageous for all involved.

Finally, using technology and online platforms can offer a way for introverts to network. Engaging in online networking enables introverts to interact with others from the comfort of their surroundings, alleviating the stress of in-person encounters. Take advantage of platforms like LinkedIn to establish connections, participate in online communities, and engage in discussions that resonate with your passions. Moreover, consider arranging one-on-one meetings or casual coffee chats instead of attending large networking events. These smaller and more personal settings create opportunities for authentic connections to blossom.

By exploring these networking strategies that play to introverted strengths, you can navigate the networking experience with quiet confidence and genuine connection. Remember to focus on your passions and interests, leverage your reflective nature, and utilize online platforms and one-on-one settings. These strategies will help you build genuine connections that align with your values and interests, leading to long-lasting and mutually beneficial partnerships.

NETWORKING IS FOR INTROVERTS TOO!

Networking might seem daunting to introverts, but it doesn't have to be that way. By using the right strategies, introverts can actually thrive in networking by tapping in to their unique strengths. In this section, we will delve into networking strategies that cater to the strengths of introverts, nurture genuine relationships, and create comfortable networking experiences. By embracing these methods, introverts can establish authentic connections and achieve networking success that resonates with their values and passions. Let's explore how you can harness your introverted nature to shine in the world of networking.

Networking is about quality over quantity. It's not about gathering a bunch of business cards or going to every networking event in town. The real secret to building a strong network lies in nurturing genuine relationships based on common interests and values. These connections are not only more meaningful but also have a higher chance of resulting in beneficial partnerships and collaborations.

Connecting with someone who has similar interests can help strengthen a bond and make you feel more comfortable around them. When two people have shared hobbies, passions, or life experiences, building a connection becomes effortless. Identifying these points can serve as a starting place for connections and further growth.

When engaging in networking, it's crucial to be genuine and open in your interactions. Share your interests, values, and experiences authentically while also being an active listener. This creates a sense of trust and allows for deeper connections to be formed. It's important to show your true self rather than put up a front or solely focus on impressing others with achievements or qualifications.

Attending networking events and conferences provides a chance to connect with people who share interests and values. It's more than swapping pleasantries and moving on to the next person. Make sure to engage in discussions and take the time to get to know the person on a deeper level. Ask open-ended questions, actively listen, and show sincere curiosity in their thoughts and experiences.

In addition to attending in-person networking events, utilizing online platforms can also serve as a means to foster authentic connections, as previously mentioned. For instance, LinkedIn provides the opportunity to network with industry peers, engage in groups, and participate in community dialogues. Make the most of these avenues to interact with like-minded individuals. Respond to their posts, share valuable content, and initiate connections through outreach.

Networking goes beyond receiving benefits from others. It involves nurturing connections that are mutually advantageous, rooted in trust and common values. When engaging in networking, focus on contributing to and adding to the lives of others. Seek opportunities to assist and stand by the individuals you interact with, be it by sharing resources, providing guidance, or facilitating connections. By demonstrating concern for others' well-being and achievements, you pave the way for enriching connections and promising opportunities to flow back to you naturally.

In summary, creating connections based on shared interests and values is crucial for effective networking. When approaching networking, be authentic, open, and genuinely interested in making connections and contributing positively to others' lives. By focusing on quality relationships over quantity, you can establish a solid network of authentic connections that may result in long-lasting and mutually advantageous collaborations.

Let's nurture our relationships with authenticity and empathy. Let's seek out those shared interests and values that form the foundation of meaningful connections. And let's approach networking as an opportunity to give and add value to others, rather than just focusing on what we can get. By doing so, we will forge authentic connections that can revolutionize our personal and professional lives.

EMBRACE AUTHENTIC NETWORKING

In the quest for meaningful connections, it's crucial to adopt networking strategies that align with your introverted strengths. By recognizing and leveraging your unique qualities, you can establish genuine relationships that are based on authenticity and compatibility. Focus on building a few strong connections rather than spreading yourself too thin.

Crafting genuine connections is the cornerstone of successful networking, especially for introverts who thrive on meaningful interactions. **Moving beyond surface-level small talk and fostering authentic relationships rooted in shared interests and values** creates a foundation for long-lasting partnerships that enrich both your personal and professional lives.

Here's how introverts can excel at building authentic connections:

1. **Seek Common Ground:** The key to any strong relationship is finding that point of connection. Look for shared interests, hobbies, or even similar professional experiences that can spark genuine conversation. **Active listening** is key—inquire about their passions and experiences and use those points of commonality to build rapport.

2. **Initiate Deeper Conversations:** Move beyond the typical 'What do you do?' questions. **Prepare conversation starters** that delve deeper into interests, values, and goals. Ask insightful questions about their work, their motivations, or their current projects. This demonstrates your genuine interest and allows for a richer exchange.

3. **Embrace Authenticity and Vulnerability:** Don't be afraid to show your true self in networking interactions. Share your own passions, experiences, and even challenges in a way that feels comfortable. **Vulnerability fosters trust and**

creates a space for genuine connection. People connect better with those who are real and relatable.

4. **Focus on Quality Over Quantity:** Don't overwhelm yourself trying to meet everyone in the room. Instead, prioritize having a few meaningful conversations with people you genuinely connect with. This allows you to build deeper connections that are more likely to be mutually beneficial.

5. **Follow Up and Show Interest:** Don't let the conversation end after the initial meeting. Send a personalized follow-up email within 24-48 hours, referencing specific things you discussed. This demonstrates your continued interest and opens the door for future interactions.

By utilizing these strategies, introverts can navigate the often-daunting world of networking with confidence, building authentic connections that lay the foundation for long-term success.

Meryl Streep, the actress known for skillful performances, is a great illustration of an introvert who excels at developing meaningful connections. During an interview, Streep expressed her preference for intimate gatherings and personal discussions, where she can genuinely engage with people on a personal level. This strategy has enabled her to establish a circle of contacts in the entertainment field while remaining authentic to her personality.

NURTURE RELATIONSHIPS FOR LONG-TERM SUCCESS

Building genuine connections is the foundation of successful networking, but the journey doesn't end there. Here's how to cultivate and maintain these relationships for long-term benefits:

- **Personalized Follow-ups:** Don't let the initial conversation fade into oblivion. Send a personalized email within 24-48 hours after meeting someone. Reference specific points from your conversation, like a shared interest or a challenge they mentioned. You can offer additional resources, ask follow-up questions, or simply express your desire to stay connected.

- **Scheduling Regular Check-ins:** Avoid the dreaded "networking black hole" by scheduling regular check-ins. Coffee chats, virtual meetings, or even quick phone calls can keep the conversation flowing and maintain a sense of connection. Aim for quarterly or bi-annual check-ins, depending on the strength of the connection.
- **Offering Support and Sharing Opportunities:** Networking is a two-way street. Look for ways to support and add value to the lives of your network contacts. Share relevant articles, job postings, or industry news that might benefit their interests. Make introductions to others in your network if you see a potential for collaboration.
- **Staying Engaged:** Social media can be a powerful tool for maintaining connections. Actively engage with your network contacts' online profiles. Like, comment on, and share their content to demonstrate your ongoing interest. This keeps you top-of-mind and fosters a sense of camaraderie.
- **Celebrating Milestones:** Take a moment to acknowledge and celebrate your network contacts' successes. A quick congratulatory message on a promotion, new venture, or even a birthday can go a long way in strengthening the bond.

HARNESS THE POWER OF ONLINE PLATFORMS

Online platforms provide introverts with a comfortable space to connect and network without the pressure of face-to-face interactions. We discussed this earlier, but let's dig a bit deeper. By utilizing these tools effectively, you can expand your network and foster valuable relationships in a setting that suits your preferences. *Leverage one-on-one settings* to deepen these connections further and create a strong support system for your personal and professional growth.

Here are some examples of online platforms that cater to introverted networking preferences:

- **Professional Networking:** LinkedIn Groups focused on specific industries or professions.
- **Interest-Based Communities:** Online forums or social media groups dedicated to shared hobbies or passions (e.g., book clubs, photography groups).
- **Mentorship Platforms:** Platforms connecting introverts with mentors who can offer guidance and support (e.g., Lunchclub, Mentored).

In the realm of networking, remember that authenticity and shared values are the keys to forging lasting relationships. By embracing your strengths, cultivating genuine connections, and utilizing online platforms wisely, you can navigate the networking landscape with confidence and create a network that truly supports and inspires you.

NEXT UP

As we conclude our exploration of introverted networking strategies, it's important to recognize that embracing your authentic self is the foundation for success in all aspects of life, including networking. By understanding and leveraging your unique strengths as an introvert, you can navigate the networking landscape with greater ease and confidence.

But the journey doesn't stop there. In the next chapter, we'll dive deeper into the concept of redefining introversion and how it can revolutionize not only your approach to networking but your entire perspective on personal and professional growth. We'll explore how embracing your introverted nature can help you thrive in a world that often favors extroversion and how you can inspire others along the way.

Imagine a networking event where you confidently share your ideas, connect with like-minded individuals, and leave feeling energized rather than drained. By redefining introversion and recognizing the power of your quiet strength, this vision can become a reality.

As we move forward, let's shift our focus to the transformative power of redefining introversion. In the next chapter, we'll explore how owning your introverted identity can lead to greater self-acceptance, improved relationships, and a more fulfilling life overall. We'll also delve into the concept of the "positive plan," a roadmap for introverts to harness their strengths and achieve their goals in a way that feels authentic and energizing.

Are you ready to embark on a journey of self-discovery and empowerment? Let's turn the page and explore how redefining introversion can help you not only navigate the networking world with confidence but also unlock your full potential in every area of your life.

CHAPTER 10

REDEFINING INTROVERSION: YOUR PATH TO THRIVING

The sunlight tiptoed through the open window, casting a warm glow on the quiet corner where Eleanor sat surrounded by the high walls of books in the town's small library. She relished this solitude, her own little bastion of calm away from the bustling world outside that seemed tailor-made for those of a louder disposition. Her eyes lingered on a page that spoke of embracing introversion, a message resonant with the unspoken yearnings of her heart.

She paused, her mind meandering to the company meeting just the day before. Eleanor had sat there, her ideas nestled in the corners of her throat, unvoiced. It felt like a room where extroversion was the only currency of value. Now the book in her lap whispered of a hidden strength, and she wondered if perhaps her gentle voice could still command a room without needing to shout.

Outside, the sounds of the world carried on, children laughing as they chased each other around the maple tree set proudly in the park. A dog barked as people's footsteps paired with the distant hum of industry. Life was in motion, an effortless ballet she observed with introspective pause.

She remembered her grandmother's words: "Your quiet nature will move mountains in its own time, darling. Let them hear you in the softness of your approach." And it struck her, in that warm, quiet corner, that maybe inspiring others did not require loud proclamations but rather the gentle, persistent flow of water that shapes stone with unhurried grace.

Eleanor composed a mental list of items she wanted to accomplish—invisible ink on her conscientiousness of how to share her story:

- Write about her journey of self-acceptance in the local newsletter.
- Volunteer for the public speaking club, using her story to encourage other introverts.
- Start a quiet but engaging social media campaign celebrating soft-spoken successes.

A smile played on her lips as, for the first time, she saw these steps not as insurmountable peaks but as trails she was well-equipped to tread.

She pictured herself following this positive plan, a future where her strengths were not just recognized but sought after. She'd craft messages that didn't just speak but resonated, that didn't just inform but transformed. What could the world look like if those like her harnessed their introspective power for the collective good?

At that moment, a paper plane glided through the still air, landing near her feet, a child's laughter following through the open window like a beckoning. Eleanor's thoughts joined the laughter for a momentary jaunt. Birds sang in chorus, and she felt that maybe, just maybe, her silence could be as influential as their song.

Eleanor closed her book, her heart now a fluttering bird in her chest. As she walked through the library aisle, each step felt purposeful, a quiet declaration of intent. Could the stories of introverts like her, once shared, inspire even the most raucous of souls to stop and listen to the whisper of their own inner voice?

UNLOCKING YOUR INTROVERTED POTENTIAL: A JOURNEY OF SELF-DISCOVERY

Hey, fellow introverts! In the previous chapter, we discovered how to maneuver through the realm of networking by leveraging our introverted strengths and forming authentic connections. What if I shared that networking is merely scratching the surface in terms of unleashing the power of your introversion?

In our world today, it's important to reconsider how introverts are viewed, especially when extroversion is often favored. Lots of people see introversion as a flaw that needs to be fixed. However, the truth is that being introverted may actually be the key to unlocking your talents that set you apart and help you thrive in all your endeavors.

Let's dive into this chapter and uncover the treasures hidden within your introverted nature. We'll delve into your ability to think deeply and creatively, as well as your skill for nurturing close, meaningful relationships, to see how these traits can drive your personal and professional growth.

It's not just about recognizing your strengths; it's equally crucial to incorporate them and allow them to stand out. When **redefining introversion** and appreciating the power of your quiet nature, you'll discover that you possess the abilities to excel in any scenario, be it at work, in your personal relationships, or while pursuing your interests.

Are you prepared to unleash the full potential of your introverted superpowers? Let's jump in and explore how redefining introversion can expand your horizons and allow you to thrive authentically and in alignment with your true self.

EMBRACING YOUR QUIET STRENGTH

Imagine a world where your introversion is not a roadblock but your most powerful ally in achieving your dreams. This is not a far-fetched fantasy but a realistic goal that you can achieve by acknowledging and leveraging the qualities that make you uniquely you. It's time to shatter the myth that to be successful, one must be outgoing, loud, and perpetually "on." In this chapter, we'll explore how introverts can flourish in a predominantly extrovert world by harnessing the power of positive thinking.

Owning your introversion is the first step toward thriving. Embrace all those amazing qualities that come with being an introvert, like your ability to think deeply, your killer listening skills, and your natural empathy. These aren't just personality traits— they're your secret superpowers. These qualities are invaluable in forging authentic relationships and achieving professional success. By embracing the full potential of your introverted personality, you not only advocate for the value of introversion in society but also set a foundation for personal fulfillment and achievement.

LEADING BY EXAMPLE

When you're living authentically, **inspiring others** comes naturally. By sharing your journey and the methods you've employed to tackle introversion-related obstacles, you can light a path for others to follow. It's not about pretending to be someone; rather, it's about embracing yourself and demonstrating that living authentically as an introvert is not only achievable but fulfilling. Your experiences could offer hope to those who are struggling to find their way in a loud world.

UNLEASHING THE QUIET POWER WITHIN

The last part of the puzzle involves harnessing **the power of the positive plan**. This means utilizing your introverted strengths to create a forward-focused method for reaching your objectives. It's about looking within yourself to discover your unique path to success instead of trying to imitate the extroverted approach that is prevalent in our society. By merging a positive mindset with an intentional plan that aligns with your strengths, you'll find that not only can you accomplish your personal and career goals, but you can also motivate those around you to rethink the influence of introversion.

We have covered a lot of ground in this book about the many ways in which the power of positive thinking can help introverts succeed in a world that typically rewards extroversion. We are getting close to the conclusion, and it has become clear that many introverts struggle with believing in themselves as well as prospering in a fast-paced world that favors the extrovert. Going from self-doubt, procrastination, and social anxieties to confidence, meaningful connections, and personal fulfillment isn't a picnic, but it is totally doable with the right frame of mind and strategy.

This chapter ties together the main themes of the book by emphasizing the importance of owning your introverted identity, inspiring others through your journey and developing a positive action plan. By doing so, you not only unlock your potential but also contribute positively to reshaping the narrative around introversion.

Your introspective journey and the power of your quiet resolve are your strengths, not your weaknesses. By applying the insights and strategies shared in this book, you're not just surviving in a busy, socially-focused world; you're thriving on your own terms. Remember, the world needs your quiet strength, your deep thoughtfulness, and your compassionate understanding now more than ever. Let your introversion shine as a beacon of hope and inspiration for all who are still searching for their path to thriving.

Embracing your introverted nature as part of your identity goes beyond self-acceptance. It's also about recognizing the unique strengths that introverts bring to the table. As an introvert, you have a range of traits that can be leveraged to achieve both personal and professional success. By owning your introversion and championing its significance in society, you can navigate the extrovert world with assurance, genuineness, and satisfaction.

OWNING YOUR INTROVERTED SUPERPOWER AND CHAMPIONING ITS VALUE

Imagine a world where your introversion is not a roadblock but a powerful force propelling you toward your dreams. This is not a fantasy but a reality you can achieve by grasping and leveraging the qualities that make you uniquely you. It's time to dismantle the myth that success requires being outgoing, loud, and constantly "on."

Unlocking Your Inner Strength:

Owning your introversion is the first step on your journey to unlocking your potential and finding success. It involves acknowledging the multitude of strengths you possess, such as deep thinking, empathy, and listening skills. These attributes are essential for building authentic connections and excelling in your professional career. By embracing the full potential of your introverted personality, you not only highlight its importance in society but also pave the way for personal fulfillment and achievement.

Championing Introversion:

Accepting oneself is just the first step in advocating for introversion. The next step is sharing your story and the methods you've used to overcome the difficulties that come with being introverted. Living genuinely as an introvert is not only doable but also gratifying; it's not about pretending but about accepting your true nature. Those who are seeking validation in a society that frequently prioritizes extroverted traits may find encouragement in your story.

By owning your introversion and championing its value, you inspire others to embrace their authentic selves and contribute to a more accepting and supportive society worldwide that celebrates the unique strengths of all personality types.

Are you ready to embrace your introversion and unlock your inner strengths? Let's explore the beauty of owning your introverted nature.

Integrating the insights from this book into your life can truly be a life-changing journey. It's more than comprehending and embracing your introverted nature; it's also about sharing your uplifting experiences and motivating others to embrace their unique introverted qualities. Through these actions, you have the ability to ignite a chain reaction of self-acceptance and empowerment in the world.

Inspiring others can be achieved by living a life that truly represents who you are. This involves aligning your behaviors, objectives, and values with your introverted nature. It's about choosing a career path that enables you to excel in settings that respect your preference for peace and contemplation. Building deep connections that prioritize meaningful conversations is also key. Moreover, it entails dedicating moments for reflection and self-care and recognizing their significance in maintaining your wellness.

SHARING YOUR POSITIVE STORIES: INSPIRING OTHERS THROUGH YOUR JOURNEY

One of the most powerful ways to inspire others is by sharing your success stories about thriving as an introvert. By highlighting the strengths that come with introversion and showcasing how they have played a role in your achievements, you empower others to accept and embrace their own introverted nature. It's a message that resonates: being introverted is not a flaw but rather a distinctive trait that can be harnessed for growth. Your experiences hold the potential to spark optimism and positivity, encouraging others to tap into their own quiet strength.

Sharing Authentically:

Here's the key: **authenticity**. People connect with being real. Don't hold back from talking about the struggles you've had as an introvert and how you've dealt with them. When you show your vulnerabilities, it helps others see themselves in you and feel like they're not alone. You become a beacon of hope and support, showing the way for those who may be struggling with their own introversion.

Examples of Sharing Your Stories:

Let's explore some concrete ways you can share your positive stories and inspire fellow introverts:

- **Blogging or Writing:** Introverts often excel at written communication. Share your experiences and insights through a blog, online articles, or even a self-published book. This allows you to reach a broad audience on your own terms, from the comfort of your own space.
- **Public Speaking:** While public speaking might seem daunting for some introverts, even small-scale presentations or workshops can be impactful. Focus on topics related to introversion and share your strategies for success. You can also participate in online webinars or panel discussions.
- **Mentorship:** Offer guidance and support to introverts who are just starting their journeys. Share your wisdom and insights and help them develop strategies for thriving.

Consider joining online communities or mentoring programs focused on introverts.

- **Social Media:** Utilize social media platforms strategically. Share inspirational quotes, success stories of other introverts, or even snippets from your own experiences. You can create a safe and supportive online community for introverts to connect and share their stories.
- **Podcasts or Interviews:** Consider being a guest on podcasts or interviews focused on introversion. This allows you to share your story and reach a wider audience who might be interested in your perspective.

Remember, the key is to find a platform where you feel comfortable sharing your voice. By offering your unique perspective and insights, you can empower others to recognize their introversion and thrive in their own way.

Here are some tips for inspiring others to embrace their introverted nature:

1. **Show, don't tell:** Instead of simply telling others to acknowledge their introversion, show them through your actions and stories. Lead by example and let your success speak for itself.
2. **Listen actively:** Practice active listening in your interactions with others. By listening attentively and empathetically, you not only make others feel heard and valued, but you also demonstrate the power of introverted strengths such as reflection and deep understanding.
3. **Share your growth journey:** Talk about the specific ways in which you've grown as an introvert. Share the strategies and tools that have helped you chart your course in an extrovert-driven environment with openness and honesty. Be open about the setbacks and challenges you've encountered along the way, as these can often be the most inspiring parts of your story.

4. **Be a mentor**: Offer guidance and support to those who are struggling with their introversion. Share your wisdom and insights and help them develop strategies for thriving as introverts. Be a source of encouragement and inspiration, reminding them of their innate strengths and unique perspective.

By incorporating these suggestions into your routine, you have the potential to inspire those around you. Whether by sharing your positive stories, offering advice to fellow introverts, or demonstrating the power of introversion in your daily interactions, your influence can truly leave a mark. Keep in mind that recognizing introversion goes beyond personal growth; it plays a role in fostering a more accepting and empathetic world for introverts everywhere.

Being an introvert and planning for success requires recognizing and utilizing your strengths. Optimize your introverted qualities and approach situations with a positive mindset. This will enable you to navigate through the challenges of an extroverted landscape with confidence and authenticity. In this concluding part of the book, we will explore the power of the positive plan, which aims to assist you in creating a roadmap for achieving your personal and professional goals.

POWER OF THE POSITIVE PLAN

Creating a positive plan involves acknowledging and espousing your strengths as an introvert. Being an introvert indicates that you have attributes like deep thinking, active listening, and the capacity to sustain focus for long durations. These characteristics can prove beneficial, as they enable you to analyze complex problems, brainstorm creative solutions, and excel in tasks that require concentration and attention to detail.

To harness the power of your strengths, it's essential to establish clear goals that align with your introverted nature. Dedicate some moments to contemplate your interests, values, and future goals. Which tasks or pursuits bring you the most satisfaction? What influence do you hope to have on those around you? By answering these questions, you can develop a plan that guides you on a personal journey that genuinely connects with your introverted identity.

When creating your positive plan, it's also important to consider your energy management. Introverts naturally gain energy from solitude and quiet reflection, while social interactions and external stimuli can drain them. To blossom in a world that equates success with being a social butterfly, it's essential to prioritize self-care and create a balanced routine that allows for ample time alone to recharge. Building periods of solitude into your schedule will enable you to show up as your best self and fully engage with the world when needed.

To unlock your potential and maintain your energy, cultivating a positive and optimistic mindset is also crucial. Rather than seeing your introverted nature as a drawback, reframe it as a superpower that sets you apart. Hold close the qualities that define you and recognize the value you bring to any scenario. By adopting this positive perspective, you will motivate others and create a culture that appreciates introversion.

Share your positive stories with others to boost your impact. Talk about how being an introvert has helped you succeed and the strategies you've used to inspire and assist introverts. Whether it's through writing, speaking, or mentoring, your genuine voice and helpful guidance can make a difference in people's lives.

As you develop your power of the positive plan, keep in mind that success looks different for everyone. Define what success means to you and craft goals that are aligned with your values and passion. Stay true to yourself and focus on progress rather than perfection. With a forward-focused plan that emphasizes your introverted strengths and a positive outlook on the world, you can navigate any challenge with confidence and create a life of fulfillment and purpose. Let's recap:

Owning Your Introversion: Consider the full potential of your introverted personality as a valuable tool for success in a world that often praises extroversion. *By owning your introversion, you unlock a world of opportunities where your unique traits shine brightly, enabling you to achieve your goals with authenticity and confidence.*

Inspiring Others: Spread some positivity by sharing your uplifting experiences and wisdom to encourage other introverts to acknowledge their true selves. *By showcasing your journey and the power of positive thinking, you can uplift others and cause a wave of self-acceptance and empowerment within the introverted community.*

The Power of the Positive Plan: Utilize your introverted nature to strategize for success in both your professional and personal lives. *By embracing your qualities and staying optimistic, you may inspire those around you and set the stage for a fulfilling future.*

Appreciating your introverted nature is not about conforming to societal norms but about celebrating your unique qualities and leveraging them for personal growth and success. In a world that often favors the loudest voices, introverts possess a wealth of untapped strength and wisdom. Remember, your introversion is not a limitation but a superpower waiting to be unleashed. Let the power of positive thinking guide you on your journey to thriving authentically and confidently in an extrovert world.

NEXT UP

As we conclude our exploration of redefining introversion and unlocking the quiet power within, I hope you now have a deeper appreciation for your introverted strengths and the incredible potential they hold. By embracing your authentic self and harnessing the power of positive thinking, you are well-equipped to navigate any challenge and create a life of purpose and fulfillment.

But this is just the beginning of your journey. The tools and insights you've gained from this book are your companions as you continue to grow, learn, and make a positive impact on the world around you.

As we step into the epilogue, let's reflect on the key lessons we've learned and explore how we can carry the power of optimism and the strength of our introverted nature into the future. Together, we'll discover how to continue this transformative journey beyond the pages of this book, embracing the boundless potential that lies within each of us.

HARNESSING OPTIMISM AND IGNITING YOUR INTROVERTED POWER

As we conclude our transformative journey together, I want to remind you of the immense power that lies within you—the power of your introverted mind and the strength of your optimistic spirit. When we first embarked on this path, we acknowledged the challenges introverts often face in a world that frequently celebrates extroversion. We recognized the pressure to conform and the feeling of being overshadowed in a society that sometimes overlooks the quiet brilliance of introverted minds.

Throughout this book, we have explored how positive thinking and optimism can empower introverts to thrive in an extroverted world. We have discovered that by embracing our unique strengths, challenging limiting beliefs, and cultivating a growth mindset, we can unlock our boundless potential and create a life of purpose and fulfillment.

In the introduction, I shared my personal journey of growing up as an introvert and feeling overshadowed by those who shone brightly in the spotlight. It was through the shared experiences and struggles of fellow introverts that I found the inspiration to write this book. My goal was to provide a beacon of hope and a toolkit for thriving, drawing from the insights of positivity and the wisdom of successful introverts who have made their mark.

As we've navigated through these chapters, we've learned to reframe our thoughts, focus on our strengths, and connect with a mindset of optimism and growth. We've explored the transformative power of gratitude, mindfulness, and self-compassion and discovered how these practices can help us overcome negative self-talk and cultivate a more positive and empowering outlook.

But the impact of harnessing optimism as an introvert goes beyond personal transformation. By embracing our authentic selves, leveraging our unique strengths, and radiating positive thinking, we have the power to inspire and influence those around us. We can lead with quiet confidence, build deep and meaningful connections, and contribute to positive change in our families, communities, and the world at large.

As you embark on the next chapter of your journey, remember to carry the lessons of this book with you. Harness the power of optimism, express gratitude for your blessings, and focus on your strengths. When faced with challenges or setbacks, approach them as opportunities for growth and learning. And always treat yourself with kindness and compassion, remembering that your introverted nature is a gift to be celebrated.

Your quiet strength, profound insights, and compassionate heart are the very qualities the world needs most. So go forward with unwavering confidence, knowing that you have the power to redefine success on your own terms and create a life of boundless potential.

In the introduction, I invited you to join me on this journey of exploration, with the promise that by the end, you would possess the tools to foster a positive mindset, overcome self-doubt and anxiety, and unlock your true potential. As we close this book, I hope that you feel empowered, inspired, and equipped with the strategies and perspectives needed to thrive as an introvert in an extrovert world.

Remember, you are part of a community of introverts who are harnessing the power of positive thinking to create positive change, one optimistic thought at a time. Together, we can shape a world that celebrates and values the quiet strength and profound contributions of introverted minds.

Now that you've reached the end of this transformative journey, I invite you to take action and implement the strategies you've learned. Start by setting three specific goals for the next month, focusing on areas where you want to apply the power of positive thinking and harness your introverted strengths. These could be related to your personal life, professional development, or social interactions. Write these goals down and place them somewhere you'll see them daily, as a reminder of your commitment to growth and self-discovery. Share your goals with a trusted friend or family member who can support you and hold you accountable.

In closing, I leave you with the luminous words of Eleanor Roosevelt:

"With the new day comes new strength and new thoughts."

Thank you for embarking on this transformative journey with me. May you always look on the bright side, embrace the power of your introverted nature, and let your optimistic spirit guide you to a future of boundless potential. The best is yet to come.

RESOURCES

Podcasts:

- "The Introvert, Dear Podcast"

- "The Introverts Edge with Rob Stone"

- "The Introvert Entrepreneur"

Online Communities:

- Introvert, Dear (introvertdear.com)

- The Strategic Introvert (thestrategicintrovert.com)

- Reddit Introvert Community (reddit.com/r/introvert)

THANK YOU

Dear Reader,

Thank you for joining me on this journey! I hope you found *Positive Thinking for the Introvert* insightful and empowering. Remember, you have within you the strength to thrive as an introvert in an extrovert world.

Claim Your Free Introvert Power Toolkit!

Don't forget to download your complimentary "**Introvert Power: Positive Affirmations**" list. Visit the link below or scan the QR code to access your gift.

https://BookHip.com/WVJBAFT

Share Your Thoughts:

I'd be incredibly grateful if you would leave a review on Amazon for this book. Your feedback helps me reach more introverts who are ready to grab their power!

The best to you,

Chloe Bryant

ABOUT THE AUTHOR

Meet Chloe, an accomplished introvert with a unique blend of expertise in business and a passion for helping and empowering others. Drawing upon her own experiences navigating the challenges and triumphs of embracing an introverted nature, Chloe has developed a deep understanding of the transformative potential of positive thinking for introverts.

With a successful career spanning over three decades, Chloe brings clarity and insight to her writing. As an avid reader and lifelong learner, she discovered the immense potential of self-help literature, particularly for introverts.

Through her own journey of self-discovery and personal growth, Chloe has distilled her knowledge into a practical and engaging guide. With wisdom, humor, and relatability, she creates a warm and inviting space for readers to explore their potential and embrace their authentic selves.

Made in the USA
Middletown, DE
06 August 2024

58626924R00080